Shells

Shells

Philippe Bouchet

Photographs by Gilles Mermet

Abbeville Press Publishers
NEW YORK   LONDON

Muséum national d'histoire naturelle
PARIS

Front cover: *Chicoreus cornucervi.* See page 119.
Back cover: *Xenophora pallidula.* See pages 50–51.
Page 1: *Neritina communis.* See page 33.
Pages 2–3: *Architectonica maxima*
Page 4: Detail of *Aspergillum vaginiferum.* See page 8.
Below: *Turris babylonia.* See page 29.
Opposite: *Columbarium pagoda.* See pages 156–57.

Originally published in France by Imprimerie nationale Editions/
Muséum national d'histoire naturelle, Paris, 2007
Designer: Pierre Finot
Reproductions: by Terre Neuve, Arles, France

First published in the United States of America by Abbeville Press, 137 Varick Street,
New York, NY 10013.

For the English edition
Editor: Susan Costello
Copyeditor: Ashley Benning
Production manager: Louise Kurtz
Jacket design and interior typography: Misha Beletsky
Composition: Julia Sedykh
English translation: Josephine Bacon

ISBN: 978-0-7892-0989-4

First edition
10 9 8 7 6 5 4 3 2 1

Library of Congress Cataloging-in-Publication Data

Bouchet, Philippe.
  [Regard sur les coquillages. English]
  Shells / text by Philippe Bouchet ; photographs by Gilles Mermet.
    p. cm.
  ISBN 978-0-7892-0989-4 (hardcover : alk. paper)
  1. Shells--Pictorial works. I. Mermet, Gilles. II. Title.

  QL404.B6814 2008
  594.147'7--dc22

                        2008007342

For bulk and premium sales and text adoption procedures, write to Customer
Service Manager, Abbeville Press, 137 Varick Street, New York, NY 10013 or
call 1-800-ARTBOOK.

Visit Abbeville Press online at www.abbeville.com.

Contents

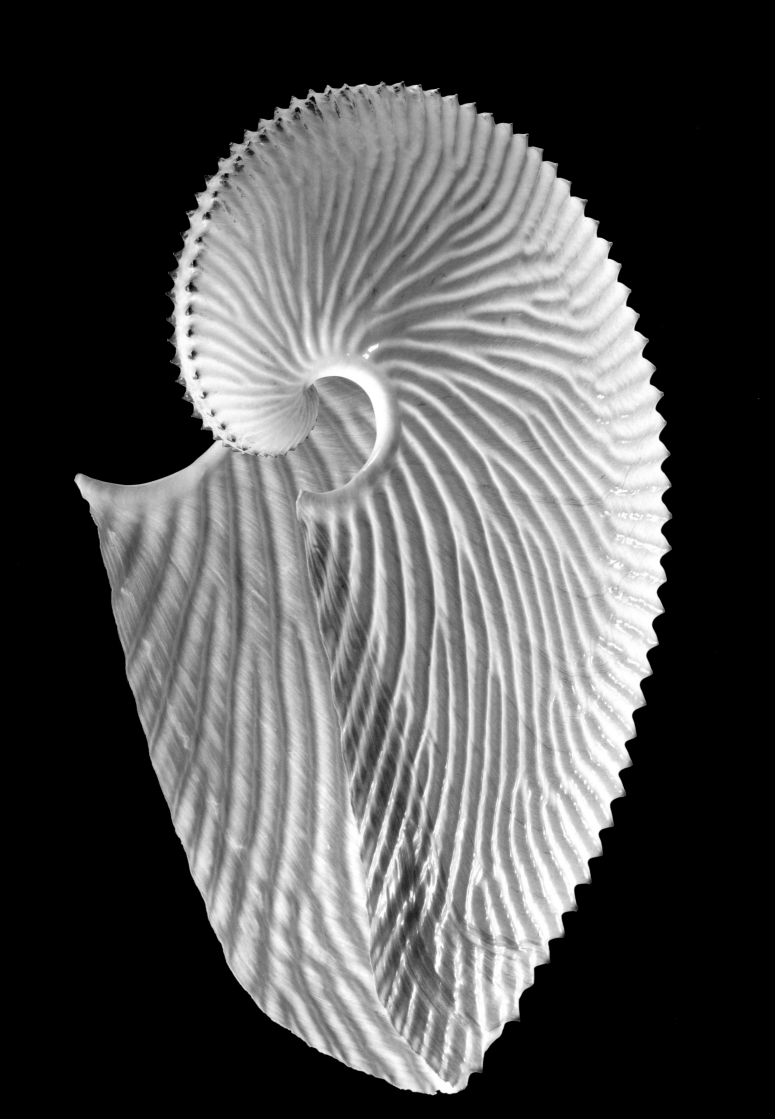

The Natural History and Artistry of Shells

◁▷
Is it or is it not a seashell?
Appearances can be deceptive in
the case of this argonaut (left),
which common sense would
certainly call a shell, whereas that
appellation would be rejected
for this misshapen watering pot
(right). Yet the former is just a
gondola secreted by a cephalopod
related to the octopus to carry
its eggs. So it isn't a seashell at
all. And yet the term seashell
is certainly applicable to the
Aspergillum vaginiferum
Lamarck, 1818 (right). It is a
bivalve that lives in tropical seas,
buried in the sand; its two valves,
which are admittedly quite small,
can still be seen in the lower part
of the tube, which constitutes a
secondary shell. The tube is open
at the top—where it pokes up
through the sand—and closed at
the other end by a filter contain-
ing minute holes that enable
water to pass through it, which
is why the ancient naturalists
gave it the common name
of watering pot.
Pacific Ocean, 185 mm (7 in.)
and Red Sea, 200 mm (8 in).

In the mid-eighteenth century, the Swedish naturalist Carl von Linné, better known as Linnaeus (1707–1778), knew of 700 species of shells; today we are aware of a hundred times more. Linnaeus classified seashells, worm tubes (serpulas), and goose barnacles in one group, and shipworms, earthworms, and leeches, in another. Nowadays, shipworms and seashells are classified in the same phylum, but barnacles are classified with crabs, and worm tubes, earthworms, and leeches are grouped together as annelids. In two hundred years, the way scientists look at shells has changed phenomenally. But has there been a change in the way collectors and artists look at them? Probably very little.

In a way, one cannot imagine more diverging views on seashells than those of Gilles Mermet and myself. As a photographer, Mermet has for this volume reviewed the collections of the Muséum national d'histoire naturelle solely on the basis of his aesthetic sense, without bothering about the names of the species he was selecting. For me, the opposite is true. The beauty of a shell is very much a subordinate consideration. As a scientist and taxonomist, the species and their names are at the core of my professional activity. Actually the word *seashell* is hardly used at all by researchers, who speak of *mollusks* and their *shells*, but leave seashells to the collectors and vacationers. Is this just a habit of speech or do shells, seashells, and mollusks actually refer to different things?

Let's begin with shells and seashells. All seashells have a shell, but not all shells are seashells. The word *seashell*

9

▽

When Édouard Lamy described these accretions in 1926 under the name of Helicostoa sinensis, *he did not know if they were tube worms or the shells of gastropods. A few years later, Alice Pruvot-Fol concluded that it was a gastropod. This weird river-dwelling gastropod had been collected from the Yangtze River in China in 1917, and has never been seen since. Its habitat was destroyed by the construction of the great Three Gorges Dam. The block measures around 25 cm (10 in.).*

▷

Tropical land snails are sometimes as brightly colored as seashells. This resemblance also reveals a common ancestry: Tortulosa tortuosa *Gray, 1847 is literally a "terrestrial seashell." In fact, unlike land snails it does not breathe through a lung; when it retracts, the animal is protected by an operculum, a horny door that closes the shell as in a winkle or a whelk. This is evidence that in the course of evolution the gastropods conquered the land not just once but several times. Thailand, about 24 mm (1 in.).*

implies something living in the sea: land snails have a shell, but this does not make them seashells. Brachiopods, Foraminifera, and sea urchins live in the sea and have shells, but are they seashells? Not really. The hard coating of sea urchins and Foraminifera are called *tests,* rather than *shells,* by scientists. As to brachiopods, ever since the classification of invertebrates separated them from the Mollusca, their exoskeleton could rightfully be called a shell, but it would be incorrect to call them seashells. In normal conversation, and despite the zoological imprecision, the word *seashell* is reserved for the external skeleton of marine mollusks. So does this mean that seashells and marine mollusks are two different names, one common and the other scientific, for the same thing? No, that isn't true either; they are not complete equivalents. Yes, all seashells are marine mollusks, but not all mollusks are seashells. For instance, nudibranchs (sea slugs) and cephalopods (octopuses and squids), to name just the main exceptions, are actually mollusks but have no exoskeleton, and so cannot be called *seashells.* Obviously, the distinction is very important for collectors, but for scientists it is less so. Collectors are categorized as interested in conchology (from the Greek *conchylios,* meaning "shell"), but scientists work in a field of zoology known as malacology (from the Greek *malakos,* meaning "soft"). So I am a malacologist, and from that point of view I am interested in mollusks, whether or not they make those shells which conchologists collect and admire for themselves.

Nearly a quarter of the species catalogued as living today on the surface of this planet are beetles (Coleoptera). Beetles live everywhere: in tropical forests, on desert scree, in caves, ponds, and rivers, on mountains and islands. In total we know of 400,000 beetle species. But since the Earth is two-thirds covered by oceans, Coleoptera actually only occupy a tiny part of the planet. Mollusks, on the other hand, are truly everywhere. They occupy the same diverse habitats as beetles but in addition also teem in coral reefs, among the offshore plankton, and in the deep abysses of the ocean. Their diversity makes mollusks the beetles of the sea. Today, nearly 60,000 species of marine mollusks are known. Add to this the 5,000 species living in freshwater and about

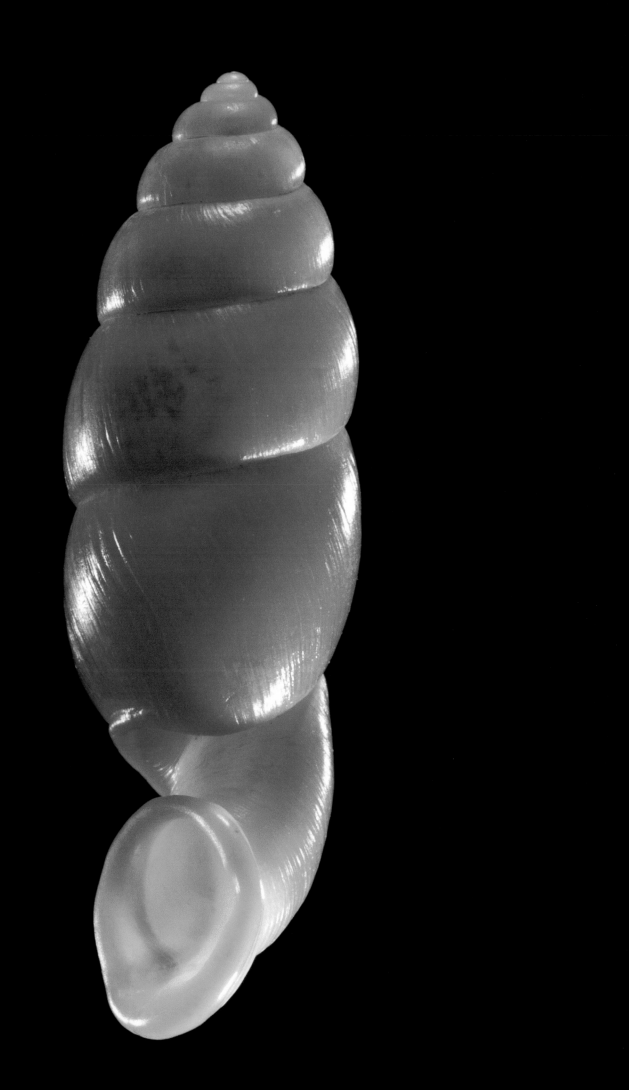

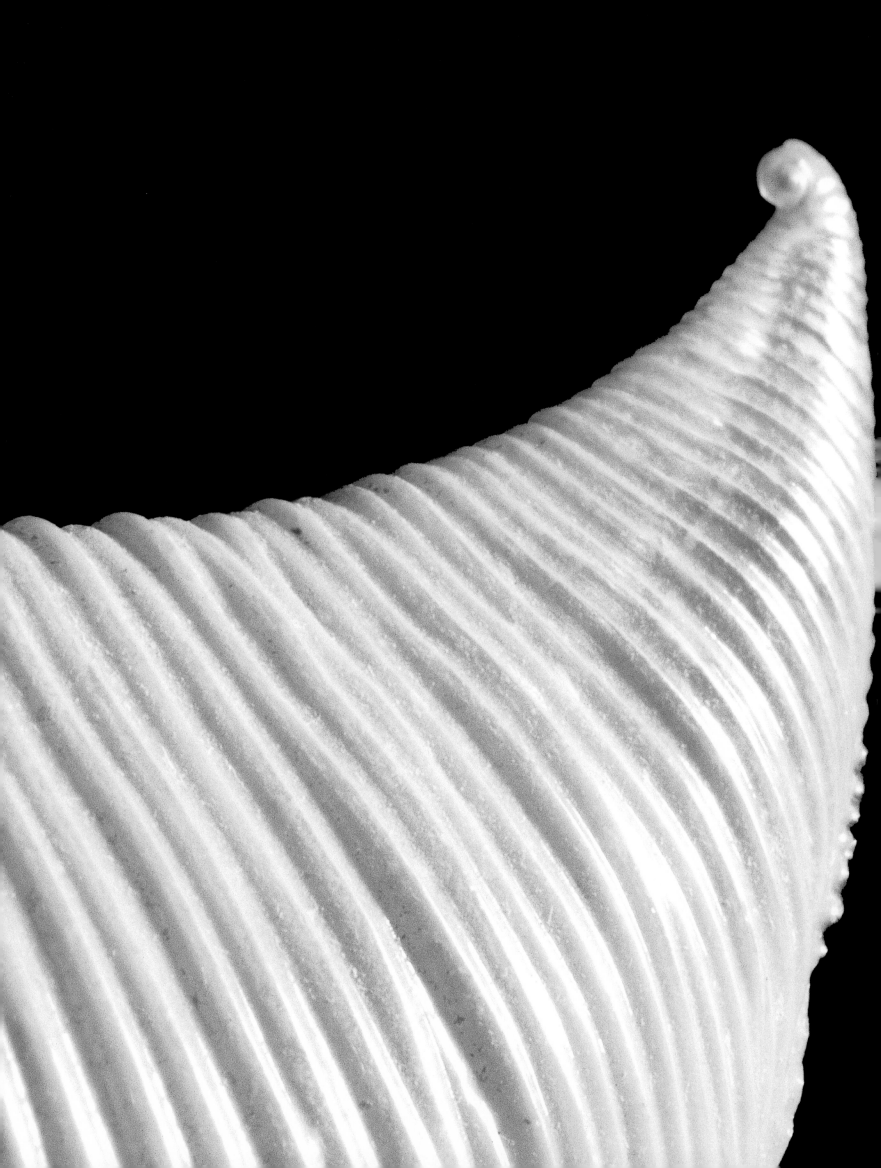

◁◁

Pages 12–14.
Carinaria vitrea *(Gmelin, 1791)*
which is not particularly prized
and somewhat neglected by
collectors today, was once one of
the most sought-after species. The
great fragility of this shell of a
planktonic mollusk results in the
extreme rarity of intact specimens.
The one illustrated here and on
the previous pages was col-
lected during the d'Entrecasteaux
expedition (1791–1794), then
passed through the hands of
Lamarck, preserved in a casket
like a precious gem.
Indian Ocean, 55 mm (2¼ in.).

▷

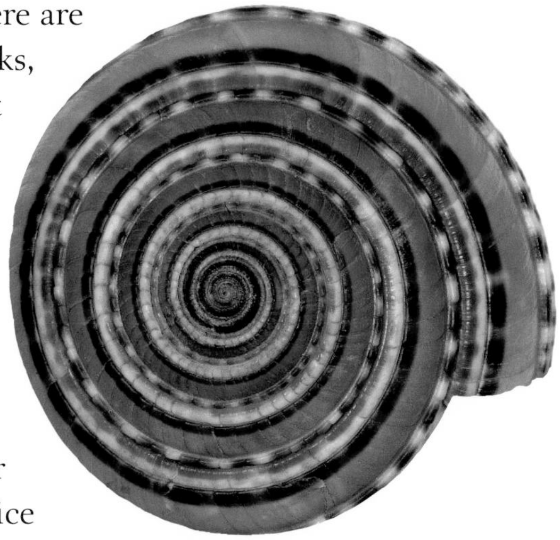

Architectonica perspectiva

▷▷

Pages 16–17.
Biplex perca *Perry, 1811.*
This ranellid shell grows periodi-
cally: at each growth stage, the
creature goes through a growth
spurt—adding half a coil in
probably just a few days—after
which it rests for several weeks
and secretes a flattened varix
(a thickened axial ridge). Varices
of successive whorls are aligned
along the spire.
Philippines, 44 mm (1¾ in.).

25,000 terrestrial snails: the known species of mollusks number no less than 90,000 species. Although they are still far behind the arthropods that crush all others by their one million species, the mollusks constitute the second-largest phylum in the animal world. In the sea, however, mollusks are the most diversified phylum: there are "only" 17,000 species of marine fish, 45,000 species of crustaceans, and 7,000 species of sponges. The smallest mollusk measures 0.7 millimeters, or just 0.03 inches, along its widest part as an adult; by contrast, the giant clam (*Tridacna*) is about one million times larger. Mollusks are also remarkable for their unbelievable diversity in terms of lifestyles and the habitats they occupy. There are herbivorous mollusks, filter-feeding mollusks, mollusks that feed on carrion, mollusks that hunt fish, others that are parasites on sea urchins, and still others that live in symbiosis with bacteria. This extraordinary diversity means that a researcher can spend an entire lifetime studying mollusks without ever completely mastering the subject.

When I am interviewed by journalists or give talks to businesses about my job, I notice a sort of ironic and condescending surprise when I admit that I do not study all ocean life, but that I am "only" a specialist in mollusks. "What a narrow specialization," I seem to read in minds and on lips. Then, when I start comparing the diversity of mollusks with that of bats (1,000 species) or birds (10,000 species), I immediately receive a little more understanding. Indeed, a malacologist specializing in cones or mussels would have to handle and study ten (or perhaps a hundred) times more species than would a mammalogist specializing in dolphins or marsupials.

Researchers study different things about mollusks. Some study, for example, the way they function, their reproduction, growth, and respiration. Others study the interactions of the species with their environment or with other species in fields such as ecology, ecotoxicology, and parasitology. Still others concentrate on the science of evolution, genetics, or paleontology, and analyze the whys and wherefores of this diversity. My speciality is the branch of biological sciences known as taxonomy, the mandate of which is to determine the frontiers between

INTRODUCTION

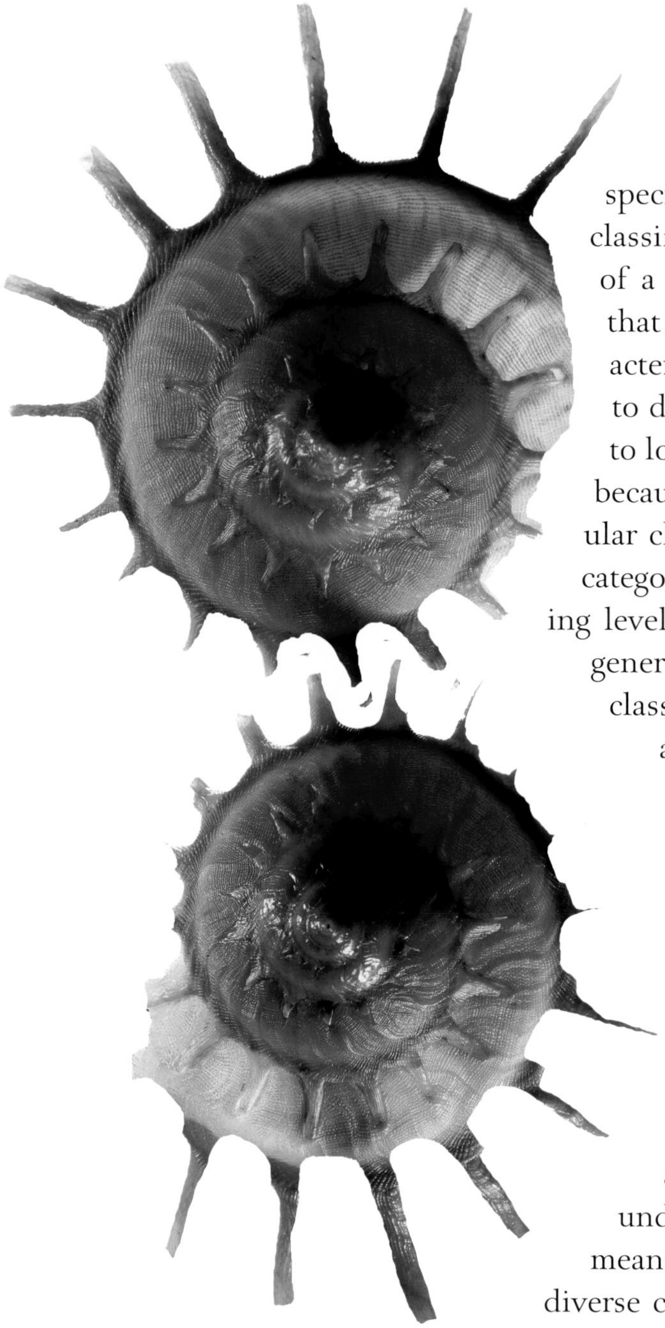

Stellaria solaris (Linnaeus, 1764).
The arrangement of these two specimens is naturally reminiscent of mechanical cogs. But it was the cosmos which inspired both Linnaeus when he established the species name solaris—*from the Latin word for "sun," of course— and Möller when he established the genus* Stellaria—*from "stars" (*stellae *in Latin). Unlike other species of the shell-carrier family (see pages 50–55) to which they belong,* Stellaria *do not carry foreign bodies on their shells. Philippines, 55 mm (2¼ in.).*

species, then to describe and name them, and finally to classify them. So my look at shells is from the point of view of a taxonomist. A taxonomist analyzes the characters that are unique to each species. These are the very characters that serve to delimit the species or in other words to define it. In addition, the job of a taxonomist is also to look for characters that are shared with other species, because it is these that will help to place them in a particular clade. The classification is organized in hierarchical categories that correspond to body structures with increasing levels of dissimilarity. Species are grouped together in genera, genera in families, families in orders, orders in classes, and classes in phyla. Mollusks, as we have seen above, are a phylum: the Mollusca. The Arthropoda (crustaceans, insects, spiders, scorpions, and so on), the Cnidaria (containing sea anemones, jellyfish, corals, sea fans, and so on), and the Echinodermata (sea urchins, starfish, brittle stars, and so on) are also phyla. Within the phylum Mollusca, taxonomists recognize eight classes: gastropods, bivalves (also known as lamellibranchs), scaphopods, polyplacophores (or chitons), cephalopods, monoplacophores, solenogasters, and caudofoveates (these last two are sometimes grouped together under the name aplacophores). Gastropods, literally meaning "crawling on their stomach," are by far the most diverse class, with just over 400 families containing 75,000 species of snails and slugs.

In view of these colossal numbers, no single book can cover all of the species of mollusks, or even all the species of seashells. Even before Linnaeus, naturalists tried to produce comprehensive monographs that would include all species known at the time. Linnaeus needed only just over a hundred pages of his *Systema Naturae* to list and describe the 700 species of shells known to him. Sixty years later, Jean-Baptiste Lamarck (1744–1829) needed two volumes of his *Histoire naturelle des animaux sans vertèbres* [Natural history of animals without backbones] to cover the 3,000 species that had been described by then. Throughout the nineteenth century, other scholars attempted the exercise. The last to do so in an authoritative way were the Ger-

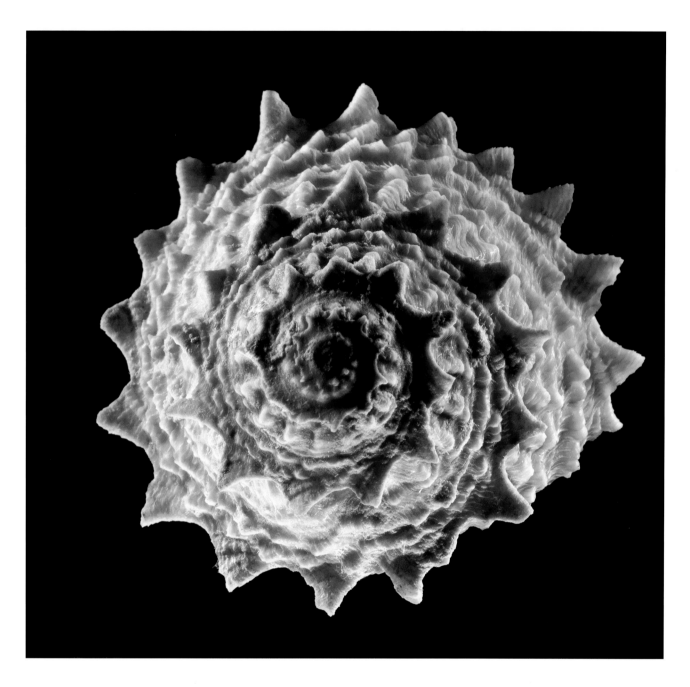

man authors of the *Systematisches Conchylien-Cabinet* and the Americans George Tryon and Henry Pilsbry, who took fifty years to publish the forty or so volumes of their comprehensive and meticulous *Manual of Conchology*. This approach to documenting the molluscan diversity of the world came to a halt in the 1910s-1920s, when it was realized that the continuous discovery of new species rendered impossible, or even futile, the printing of monumental species directories that became out of date as soon as they were published.

Pages 19–22.
*The so-called long-spined star snail (*Astralium phoebium *[Röding, 1798]) does not appear to deserve this common name except in comparison to other West Indian species of* Astralium, *the spines of which are even shorter. All are peaceful grazers on short algae in subtidal meadows and on reefs. Tropical American Atlantic, 34 mm (1½ in.).*

INTRODUCTION

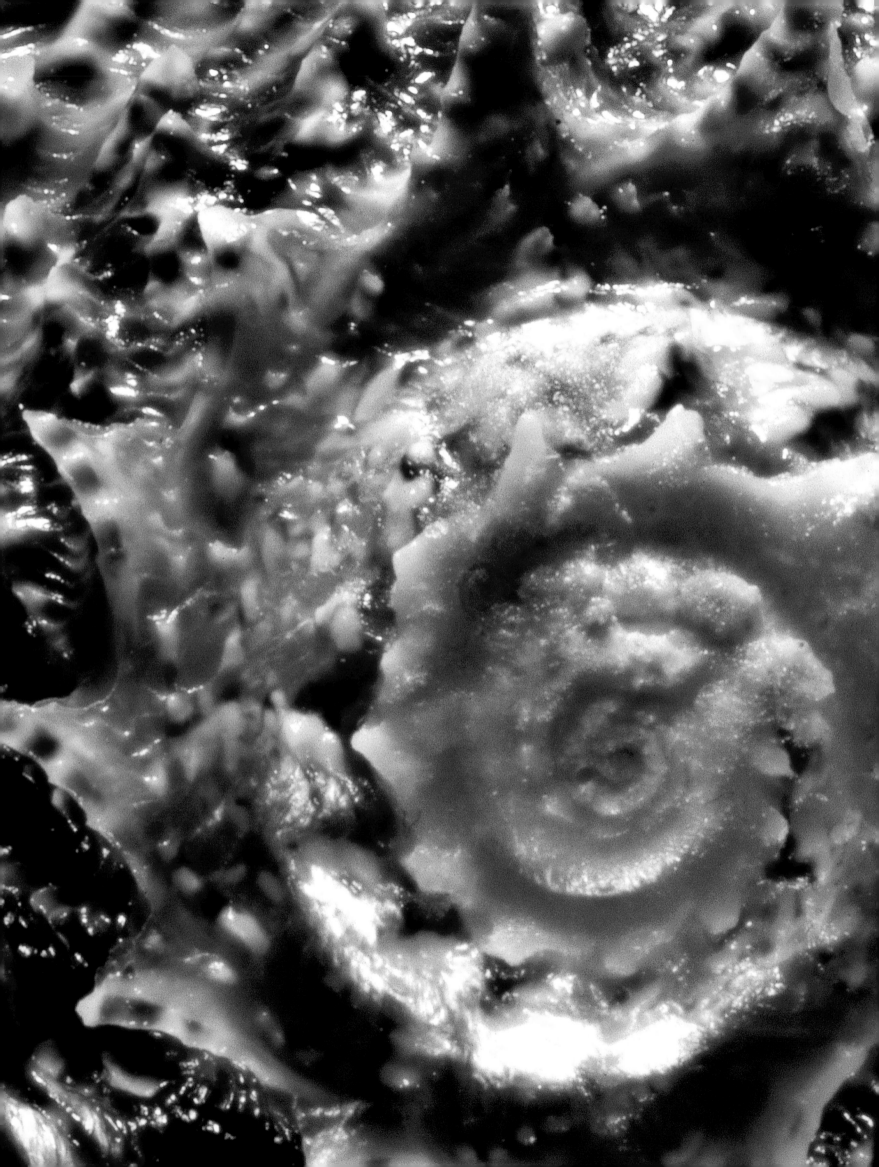

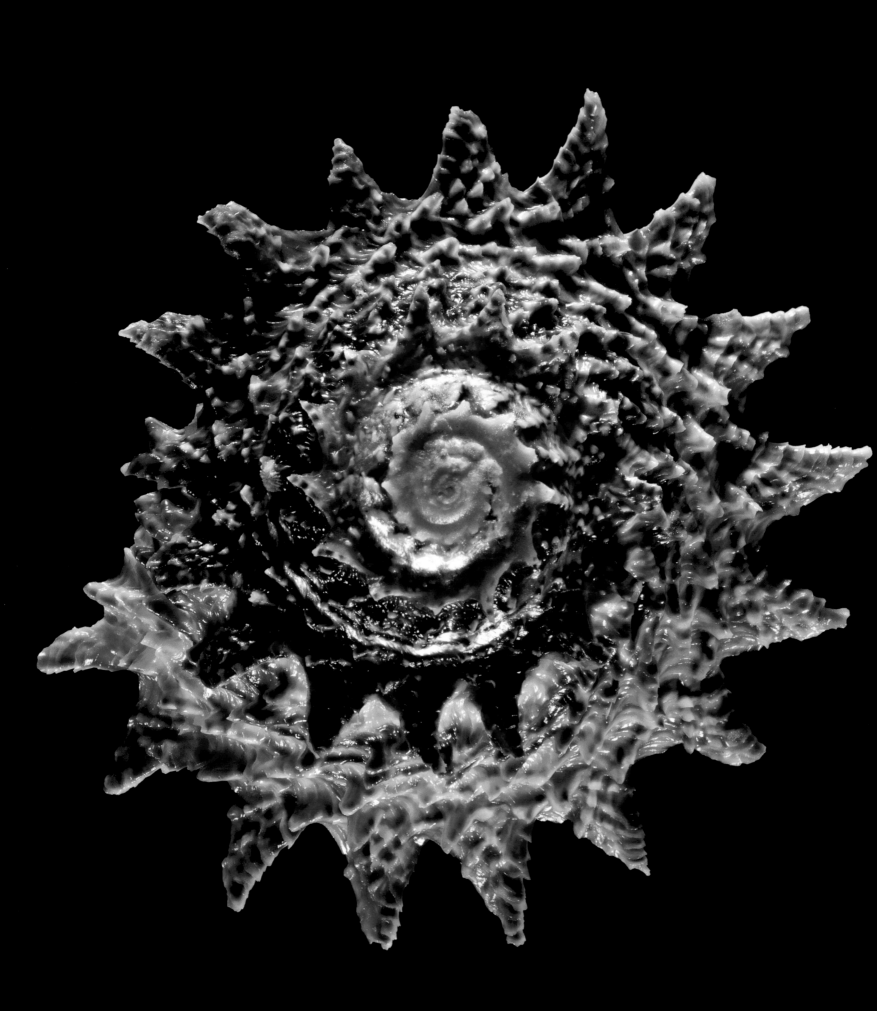

Very early on, conchologists and malacologists began publishing the results of their observations and discoveries in the form of books or brochures but, above all, as articles or notes in scientific and academic journals. As early as 1665, the Royal Society launched the *Philosophical Transactions* in London, and Denis de Sallo launched the *Journal des Savants* in Paris. Scientific societies and their publications were established in America even before the Declaration of Independence. Benjamin Franklin, among others, started the American Philosophical Society, the first American scientific society, in Philadelphia in 1743. After a brief and unsuccessful experiment in the 1770s, the first journal specifically dedicated to the study of mollusks, the *Zeitschrift für Malakozoology* [Journal of Malacozoology], went into publication in Germany in 1844. It was soon followed by the *Journal de Conchyliologie* and the *American Journal of Conchology*, which started to appear respectively in 1850 and 1865. By the late nineteenth century, the United States, Great Britain, France, Germany, and Italy all had one or more scientific publications devoted to the study of mollusks. Today, there are no fewer than fifty professional journals devoted to malacology; Japan has had one since 1928; Australia since 1957; Korea, Russia, and Poland all have their own publications. A large mollusk library thus contains several thousand books and dozens of specialist journals. The diversity of languages as a barrier to scientific communication is beginning to disappear. Although national or regional languages remain the primary vehicle for teaching and outreach, English has become the Latin of modern times when it comes to disseminating original research findings. Thus, when I communicate with the public in my country, I do so in my language, French; but when I want to be read by researchers in Singapore, Sydney, Rio de Janeiro, and Moscow, I address them in the only language that we have in common—English.

This volume, *Shells*, occupies a very minor place in the galaxy of knowledge on mollusks. It is an invitation for you to sample the joys of seashells, and while not a scientific work, it is intended to illustrate how scientists view the world of mollusks. Above all, it is an autobiographical narration about what it is like to be a malacologist and share with you a passion that has always motivated me. In this sense, and at the risk of sounding pretentious, Gilles Mermet and I would like to compare ourselves with Georg Knorr, author of a book with a truly evocative title published in Nuremberg in 1764: *Delights for the Eyes and the Spirit, or a General Collection of the Different Species of Shells That the Sea Contains.*

Above and pages 26–27.
Whether in the Mediterranean
Basin or Central America, neo-
lithic peoples had a predilection
for ornaments and decorations
cut from bivalves. Red specimens
appear to have been particu-
larly sought after. By contrast,
neolithic populations in Asia are
not known to have demonstrated
a similar interest or there is
no doubt that the regal thorny
oyster, Spondylus regius
Linnaeus, 1758, *shown above and*
on pages 26–27, would have been
greatly appreciated.
Philippines, 140 mm (5½ in.).

Opposite.
In all the temperate and
warm seas of the world, pen
shells embed themselves, point
downward, in the seabed. The pen
shell illustrated here is the amber
pen shell, Pinna carnea Gmelin,
1791. *The fan shell,* Pinna
nobilis Linnaeus, 1758, *which*
lives in the Mediterranean Sea,
was exploited by the ancients for
the threads of its byssus, which
are shiny and fine as silk and
which were woven into fabric.
West Indies, 175 mm (6¾ in.).

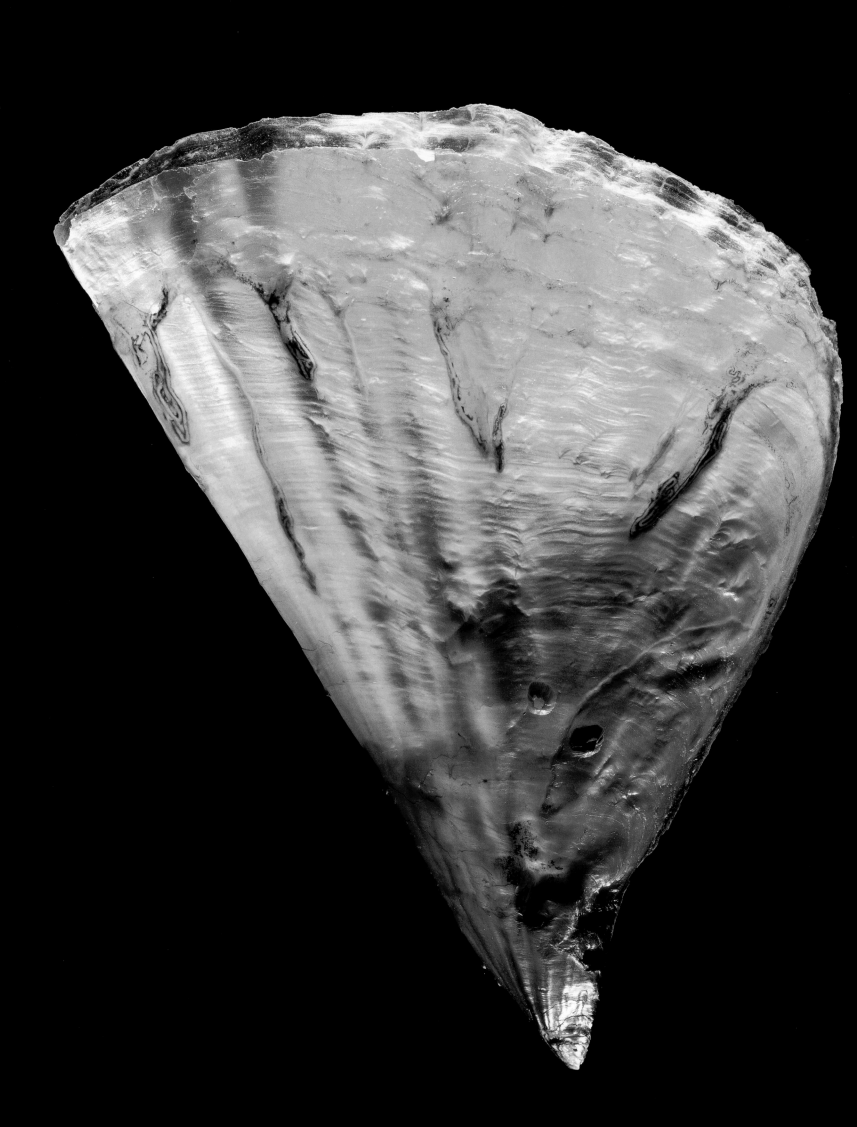

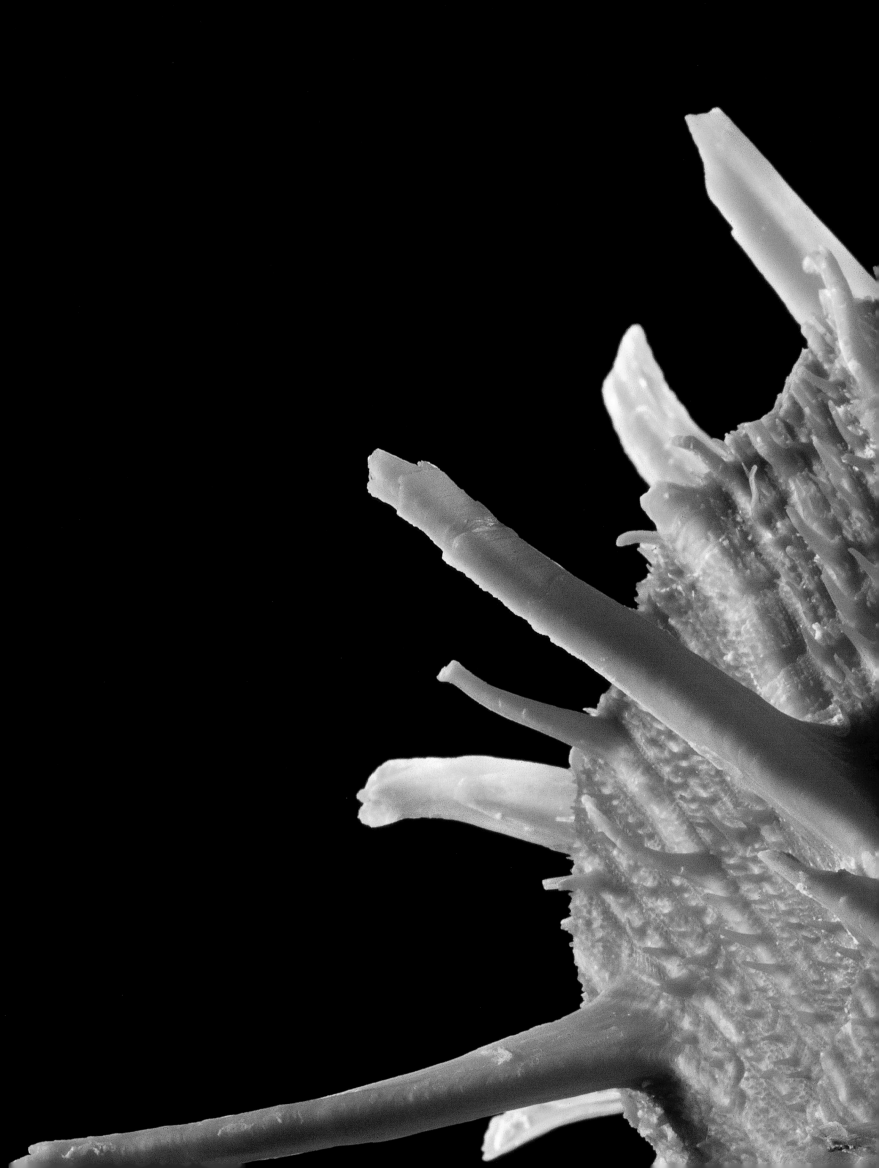

Exploration and Discovery

I never tire of telling people how exciting it is that, in this early twenty-first century, the surface of the planet still contains plants, animals, and fungi that no one has ever seen and still have no name. Our contemporaries imagine that, in the age of genetic engineering, nanotechnology, and space exploration, every nook and cranny of the globe has been mapped and its flora and fauna have all long since been thoroughly documented.

Twenty-five years ago, researchers believed that they had inventoried around 1,600,000 species, and that this figure represented perhaps half the animal and plant species on Earth. In the 1980s, new methods for sampling insects in tropical rainforests and small-sized fauna in the deep ocean led to a reassessment of this estimate. It is currently thought that 1,800,000 species have been described to date, but there remain another ten, and maybe even thirty, million yet to be uncovered. Along with this change in paradigm, inventorying biodiversity is no longer perceived as "outdated science"; it is now represented as a modern activity that is part of megascience. The reasons behind this change in attitude should probably be sought in the general anxiety caused by our perception of current climate change and unsustainable development. When these are translated into terms of scientific strategy, the feeling is that there is no time to lose if we want to discover and describe biodiversity before it disappears forever.

Outside the small community of taxonomists, it is not generally known that the discovery of new species of plants and

◁▷
The spindle shell, Turris babylonia *(Linnaeus, 1758). With more than 3,000 species already described and probably another 10,000 still to be discovered and named, the* Turridae *constitute the most diverse family of seashells. They are closely related to the cones or cone shells and, like them, have a poison gland which they use to hunt the worms on which they feed. The transverse section (left) shows the axis of the spiral, known as the "columella." Indonesia, 80 mm (3¾ in.).*

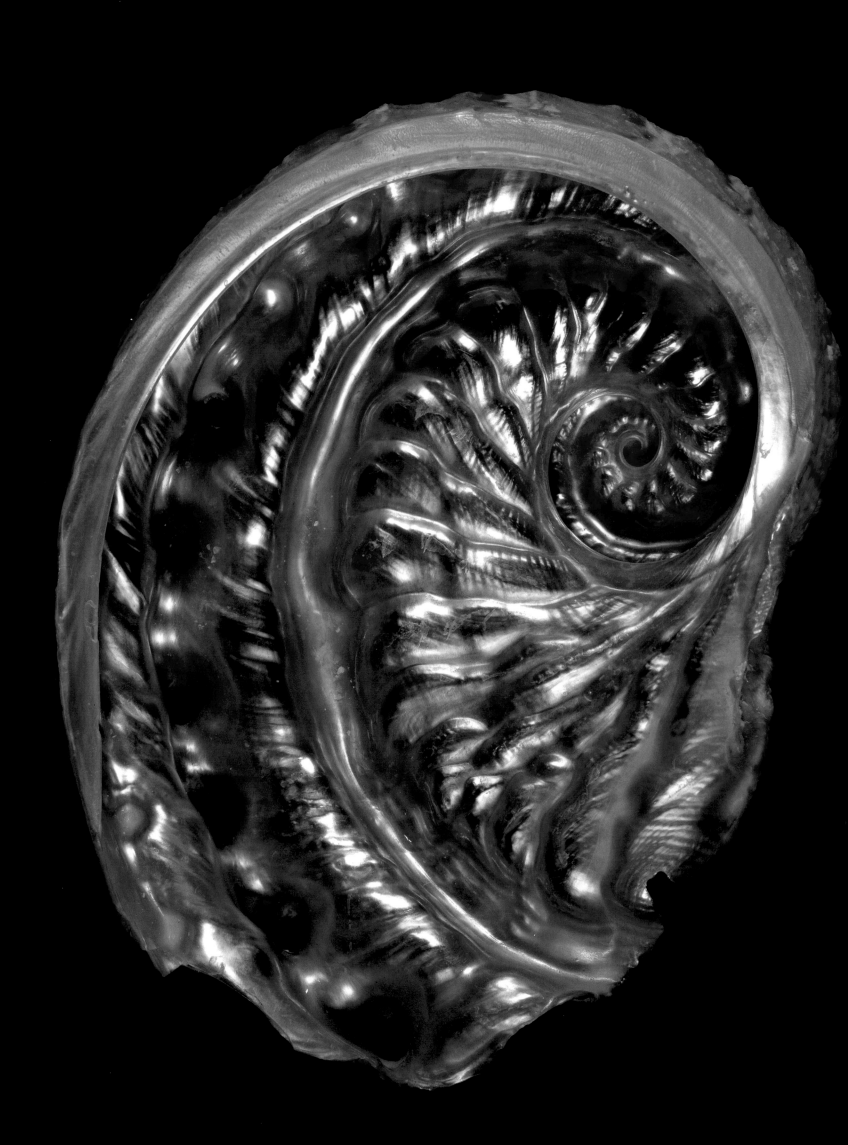

◁◁

Pages 30–31.
Haliotis scalaris *Leach, 1814.*
Warm seas are heaven for many groups of seashells, but abalones favor cold temperate waters. California, once an abalone commercial hotspot, now produces only a small fraction of its former output. In terms of diversity Australia remains the abalone capital of the world, with twenty-five recognized species. The holes are used to circulate water inside the mantle cavity of the animal; they are sealed as the animal grows, so that only the last five to seven holes remain functional.
Australia, 78 mm (3 in.).

▷

Polychromatism comes from the Greek poly "numerous," and chroma "color." If there is one shell that illustrates this type of variation within a single species, it is the zigzag nerite, Neritina communis *(Quoy & Gaimard, 1832).*
Philippines, 11–20 mm (½–¾ in.).

▷▷

Pages 34–35.
I have personally dedicated a certain number of new species to other scientists, and colleagues have also done me the honor of dedicating some to me. The one of those of which I am the most proud is Bayerotrochus boucheti *Anseeuw & Poppe, 2001, the largest of the five species of slit-shells found off New Caledonia. It lives at depths between 300 and 600 meters (roughly 1,000 to 2,000 feet) on the Norfolk Ridge, south of New Caledonia, where I first discovered it in 1985.*
New Caledonia, 95 mm (3¾ in.).

animals, far from being an exceptional event, is in fact the daily and predictable outcome of the exploration of this planet and subsequent research conducted in the laboratory. On average, as many as 16,000 new descriptions are added to the global inventory of biodiversity every year. Of course, groups that have been extensively studied, such as birds, contribute very little to this phenomenal statistic, and the discovery of every single new species of bird is indeed a significant event in ornithological circles. Insects provide the largest contingent of new discoveries. No fewer than 7,000 new species of insects are described every year by entomologists, of which 2,300 are beetles alone. Between these two extremes, the inventory of mollusks grows at an annual rate of around 570 new species, which subdivide into 350 marine species and 220 land and freshwater species.

Where do the newly discovered species come from? From distant lands and inaccessible places, you might think. Well, you would be only *partly* right. If I replied that the answer to this question is: "You find new species wherever you look for them," you might get the impression that I was making fun of you, but you would be quite wrong in that. Researchers and resources (libraries, reference collections, funds) are concentrated in developed countries such as the United States, Europe, Japan, and Australia. Historically, the temperate regions of the Northern Hemisphere have benefited from the greatest attention from naturalists, who began by making inventories of what they found on their own doorstep. This attention continues today. For an American or European researcher, it will always be easier to find funds for a project "close by," the purpose of which will be much more attractive to the national or state agencies and research programs distributing the funds. But in fact, we now know that the ecosystems of the temperate zones, although the best known, are not that rich in species, whereas the tropical ecosystems—especially rainforests and coral reefs—are teeming with a kaleidoscope of species, many of which are still unknown. We are thus in the paradoxical situation that the rich countries in the temperate regions are the best explored and continue to receive a disproportionate share of attention from researchers, while it is in the developing countries, which suffer from a deficit of knowledge, financial resources, and infrastructure to study their biodiversity, that the most discoveries remain to be made and biodiversity is also most seriously threatened. This discrepancy between resources

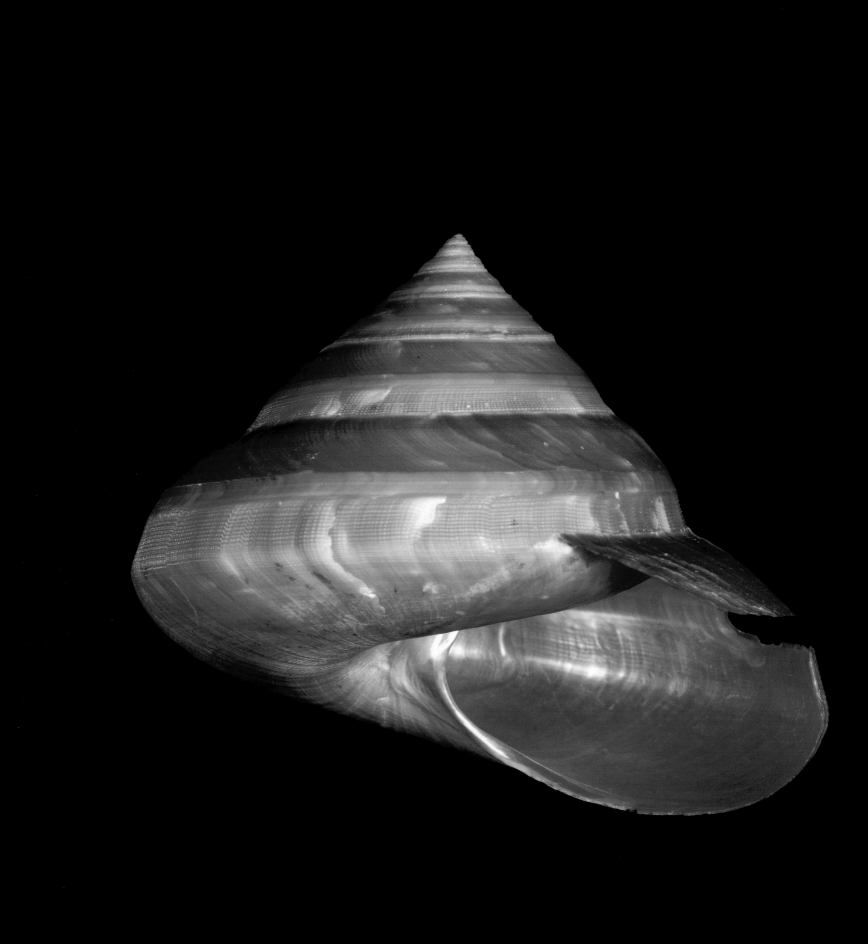

and needs is what the international Convention on Biological Diversity has recognized under the name of "taxonomic handicap." Despite this handicap and imbalance, 60 percent of newly described species of marine mollusks originate, as might be expected, from tropical seas. The Indo-West Pacific tropical region accounts for the lion's share, and this is explained by the fact that it is the richest in species and also covers the largest area. This immense biogeographical province is the main source of new marine species found today, and no doubt also the main reservoir of species to be discovered in the future. Another reservoir is constituted by the deep ocean. Sixty-five percent of the planet is covered by the sea with an average depth of more than three thousand meters (over 10,000 feet or 2,000 fathoms). The deep ocean was long regarded as a hostile environment, where only a very few species managed to survive in the icy waters, in total and constant darkness and at massive pressure, and with scant sources of food. Our vision of the abysses has now completely changed. Of course, it remains just as cold, and the darkness and heavy pressure have not changed, but our perception of the evolutionary consequences of these conditions has changed. Today, marine biologists believe that the great stability of this environment actually favors the coexistence of a large number of highly specialized species. Up until the 1960s, the huge diversity of creatures living at great depths had remained unnoticed by oceanographers because most of the species there are minute in size and many escaped a sorting process that was not careful enough. The great ocean depths certainly remain a gold mine of discoveries for the future, but their exploration is expensive and they therefore remain insufficiently studied. So we have the tropics, on the one hand, and the deep sea on the other. The combination of the two suggests that the tropical deep sea ought to be the least known environment for marine biodiversity, and that is precisely the case.

I developed a passion for zoological exploration at an early age, and as a student, my dream was to discover just *one* new species. Thirty years later, my dream has come true beyond all my hopes and expectations. Since 1985, I have teamed with Dr. Bertrand Richer de Forges, senior

◁
Glory scallop (Gloripallium pallium). *See caption on page 42.*

△
It is often said that taxonomists are an endangered species. However, the increasing accessibility of documentary resources online is making bibliographical research and examination of types much easier, and the discipline is thus being opened to a much larger number of players. More than half the new species of seashells are currently described by amateurs. One of them is Luigi Bozzetti, who since the 1980s has named several dozen new species from Somalia, the Philippines, and Madagascar. This one is Trochus ferreirai Bozzetti, 1996.
Philippines, 22 mm (1 in.)

EXPLORATION AND DISCOVERY

scientist at the *Institut de recherche pour le développement* (IRD) in Nouméa, New Caledonia, to explore the deep-sea fauna of the South Pacific. We are fortunate in having the IRD maintain in Nouméa a small, twenty-seven meter (90-foot) research ship, the R.V. *Alis*, which despite its small size is equipped with a multi-beam echosounder. A solid winch, and three to four kilometers (two to three miles) of steel cable fourteen millimeters (half an inch) thick, enable us to drop dredges and trawls down to a depth of twelve hundred meters (four thousand feet). Our first expeditions began in New Caledonia waters, within the two hundred nautical miles over which the country exercises economic sovereignty. New Caledonia and its dependancies occupy 18,000 square kilometers (6,950 square miles) of land, but the Economic Zone covers more than 1,000,000 square kilometers (400,000 square miles) of sea. The topographical features of this area include coral drop-offs, submerged ridges, guyots (flat-topped seamounts), canyons, and plains—in other words, enough to keep biologists busy for many years. We gradually extended our prospecting beyond New Caledonia to other groups of islands in the South Pacific. These were the Wallis and Futuna Islands in 1992, the Marquesas in 1997, Fiji in 1998–99, Tonga in 2000, the Solomon Islands in 2001 and 2004, and Vanuatu in 1994 and also since 2004. We embark every year on an exploration expedition of a kind that many of my colleagues in the other major museums of the world can only dream of experiencing just once in their lives, and I am aware of my living in a true "golden age" of zoological exploration.

An expedition on R.V. *Alis* consists of a team of six researchers and technicians, but the success of this type of operation is largely dependant on the skills and dedication of the ship's crew, both on deck—and in the galley. Crew members are artists capable of planting a net on a small ledge at a depth of 500 meters (over 1,500 feet), or skiing a trawl down a steep slope in 1,000 meters (3,000 feet).

◁▷
In 1988 I named this shell of the family Cassidae Cassis abbotti *in honor of the American malacologist R. Tucker Abbott, a figure famous in the world of shell collectors as well as in academia. He was the author of the reference work on the helmet shells of the world that I used to conclude that this single specimen, found off the Chesterfield Islands, in the Coral Sea, in 1984, represented a new species. Since then, although a few additional specimens have been dredged,* Cassis abbotti *remains extremely elusive. Chesterfield Islands, 43 mm (1¾ in.).*

A typical day on the *Alis* begins around 6:00 a.m. The head of the expedition draws up a program for the day, based on the results of the bathymetric survey conducted during the night and on the weather conditions. The first haul, dredge or trawl, is on board at 8:00 a.m., and six to eight successive hauls are performed until 6:00 p.m. In a successful operation, between 150 and 400 liters (150 to 400 quarts) of material are dumped on deck; they hold a hidden treasure but need to be sifted, washed, and sorted. An oceanographic expedition involves lots of work that is similar to an excavation during which tons of sediment are sieved, using a finer and finer mesh, down to one millimeter. Larger sediments of up to three millimeters (one-eight of an inch) are all sorted with the naked eye on board. The finest sediment is subjected to a "quality control" after which the decision is made as to whether to retain some, all, or none of it. That's because you don't hit a bull's-eye each time you cast your nets. The success of an expedition is based on the quality of the sorting work and the number of samples taken from the sea, but it is not unusual for a number of mediocre hauls to succeed each other, one after the other. Often the unevenness of the seabed only enables very small working areas, e.g., between 180 and 350 meters (600 to just over 1,000 feet) in one place, 250 and 400 meters (800 to 1,300 feet) in another, and 800 and 1,100 meters (2,600 to 3,600 feet) elsewhere. Yet, during an expedition typically lasting from two to four weeks, the hauls pooled together represent a comprehensive coverage of the range of depths between 100 and 1,200 meters (330 to 4,000 feet).

Although Richer de Forges specializes in crustaceans and I specialize in mollusks, our aim is to maximize the results of our dredge and trawl hauls, and thus to sort and preserve a collection that is representative of the marine fauna in its entirety; we know that we are the first, and perhaps the last in many years, to sample the area in which we sail. So we also take samples of fish, sea urchins, brachiopods, sea fans, and so on: in short, whatever the nets bring us. When we began our expeditions in 1985, the deepwater fauna of New Caledonia was terra incognita; today it has become the most thoroughly sampled tropical island in the world. This is now true of the neighboring groups of islands as well. This research program to explore the deep-water bottom fauna of

Pages 40–43.
Even a nonspecialist will instantly recognize a representative of the scallop family, or Pectinidae. All species of Pectinidae are potentially edible, but some are small, rare, and only sought by collectors. Among the 250 species are the glory scallop, Gloripallium pallium *(Linnaeus, 1758), Philippines, 62 mm (2¼ in.; page 36); the knobby scallop* Caribachlamys pellucens *(Linnaeus, 1758), Florida, 33 mm (1¼ in.; pages 40–41 and above); and* Mirapecten mirificus *(Reeve, 1853), Philippines, 37 mm (1¼ in.; page 43).*

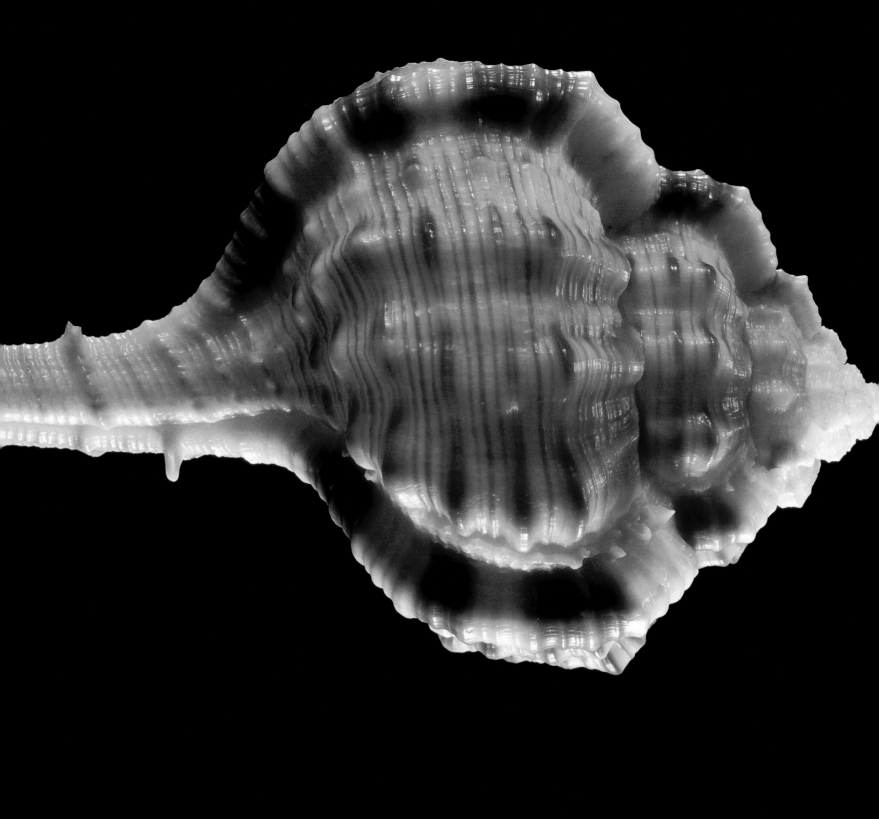

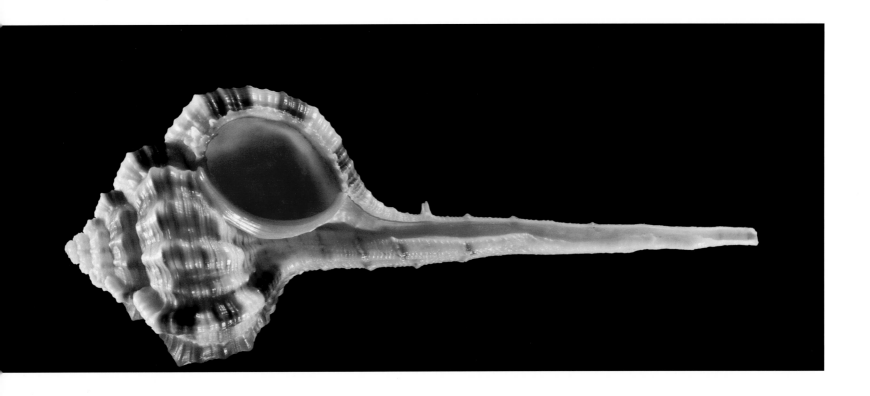

the tropical Indo-Pacific has generated the discovery of several thousand new species, in all the zoological groups, from sponges to fish, through crustaceans, echinoderms and, of course, mollusks.

Even when you are the first to trawl the seabed at 600 meters (2,000 feet), it is rare to be able to shout "Eureka!" straight from the deck of the ship. The number of known species is simply too large to be able to memorize even 10 percent of them. Of course, there are families or genera that I know better than others, but there is always the danger of forgetting one, or being carried away by performing too perfunctory an examination of the specimen, or perhaps misappreciating a variation. Nevertheless, when the dredge brought up a young specimen of a volute on Kelso Bank in the Coral Sea, I immediately realized that this was a new species. So it was indeed a "Eureka!" moment. But the volute was merely a juvenile, and although my opinion about it was unequivocal, I was not going to name a new species based on a single, non-adult specimen. For two whole days, we dredged the bottom over and over near that first spot, and for two days, we came up with nothing. Then, on the morning of the third day, on the neighboring Capel Bank, the net finally brought us a superb adult specimen, confirming the characteristics of the immature one in every respect. I named this new species *Lyria exorata*, which means "obtained through the power of prayer." Eureka! There were more "Eurekas" when we trawled up the first large slit shells on Norfolk Ridge and when we dredged the extraordinary olive shells, with their axial grooves, which I named *Entomoliva mirabilis*.

Most of the time, however, we really don't know. We see that a particular seashell is unknown to us, but that does not mean that it is a new species. Or else we see nothing at all because the seashell is too small or it has remained so briefly before our eyes. On board ship is not the place to study the samples. The expedition ends with containers full of bags and jars of spirit or formaldehyde, containing organisms sorted by phylum and duly labeled. The time all this takes to be crated up and forwarded to the museum means that the samples cannot be worked on until six months later. At that time, the chain of operations falls under the control of Philippe Maestrati, who ensures that the mollusks sampled at each station are sorted by family and stored in tubes or bags. Each specimen must be traceable to a station, a dredge or trawl haul, complete with the latitude, longitude, and depth of the site at which it was found. Finally, when all the mollusks from the expedition have been completely sorted and grouped into families— an operation that can take several months—the real taxonomic study can begin. This work is based in turn on an international network of specialists. The Muricidae (rock snails) are sent to Roland Houart in Belgium; the Eulimidae (a family of micromollusks that parasitizes starfish and sea-urchins) are sent to Anders Warén in Stockholm, Sweden; the Architectonicidae (sundial shells) go to Rüdiger Bieler in Chicago; and so on.

Taxonomy is a branch of biology in which there is little competition between researchers. There is so much to study, and in fact, there are too few of us. We, therefore, form an international network in which each has his own microspecialty. Even though Houart is not the collector of the new species of Muricidae he describes, he is their discoverer: it is he who, often two or three years after the net was opened on board ship, and knowing each of the 1,500 species of Muricidae that have already been described throughout the world, is capable of claiming: "This is a new species." "Eurekas" may be deferred in this way for a very long time. That is because there are families of mollusks for which there is no specialist anywhere in the world. Of course, it would

Lister's conch, Mirabilistrombus listeri *(Gray, 1852). All species of Strombidae were long classified in the genus Strombus. Strombids were already present in the seas of the Jurassic and Cretaceous periods, and the evolutionary history of this geologically very old family is now better known. As a result of this new understanding of the family, strombs are now split into a dozen different genera. Once considered to be very rare,* M. listeri *is a species restricted to the northern part of the Indian Ocean, where it is not rare at depths between 50 to 100 meters (140 to 330 feet). Size: 140 mm (5½ in.).*

be criminal to neglect or discard samples from such a family. They were expensive to harvest, sort, and label, and it is almost certain that there will be no opportunity to go back and catch them when someone is ready to study them. That is precisely why one of the roles of a museum is to archive such collections—as long as it takes.

In applied research, the results take the form of patents; in basic research, they take the form of papers published in academic journals. To be evaluated and validated, a discovery must be made public. When a scientist has finished a piece of research, or perhaps when he has interim results, he writes a paper that he submits for publication to the journal of his choice. In the case of malacologists, these will be specialist malacological publications, such as the *American Malacological Bulletin* or *Nautilus* in the United States, the *Journal of Molluscan Studies* in the United Kingdom, or *Venus* in Japan. The journals may also be of a more general nature, such as one covering all marine biology (for instance, the *Bulletin of Marine Science*) or one published by an institution (for instance, the *Proceedings of the Academy of Natural Sciences of Philadelphia*); finally, a research article might appear in a journal that publishes results in every field of science, from astrophysics and prehistory to genetics and chemistry. In the United States, such generalists include the *Proceedings of the National Academy of Science* or *Science*; or in the United Kingdom, *Nature*. Altogether, there are several thousand scientific journals in the world.

So how does a researcher choose where to publish his material? Researchers are guided in their choice by two fundamental criteria: relevance and reputation. Relevance comes into play because in this multitude of journals, a researcher will consider that his results might be more widely read by the colleagues he wants to reach in a particular journal rather than in another. Reputation applies because, for a professional scientist, it is more prestigious to publish in certain "major" journals than in other "minor" ones. In this respect, *Science* and *Nature* are, in some ways, the Holy Grail of every researcher. Being published in either of them is an achievement that is likely to bring honor, promotion, and funding. So why doesn't everyone send papers to these famous journals? Well, in fact, many scientists do attempt to do so, but the competition is fierce. These high profile journals only publish outstanding results that are liable to be of interest to a large swathe of the scientific community, such as the successful cloning of a monkey, the discovery of a material that can act as a superconductor at ambient

The Muricidae, or murex shells, are not only built on the "sharp and pointed spines" model (pages 154–55), they also exist in the "aerial blades or wings" model. Pterynotus elongatus (Lightfoot, 1786) owes its name (from the Greek pteros, "wing") to the regularly spaced blades that give it grace and elegance. Philippines, 62 mm (2½ in.).

EXPLORATION AND DISCOVERY

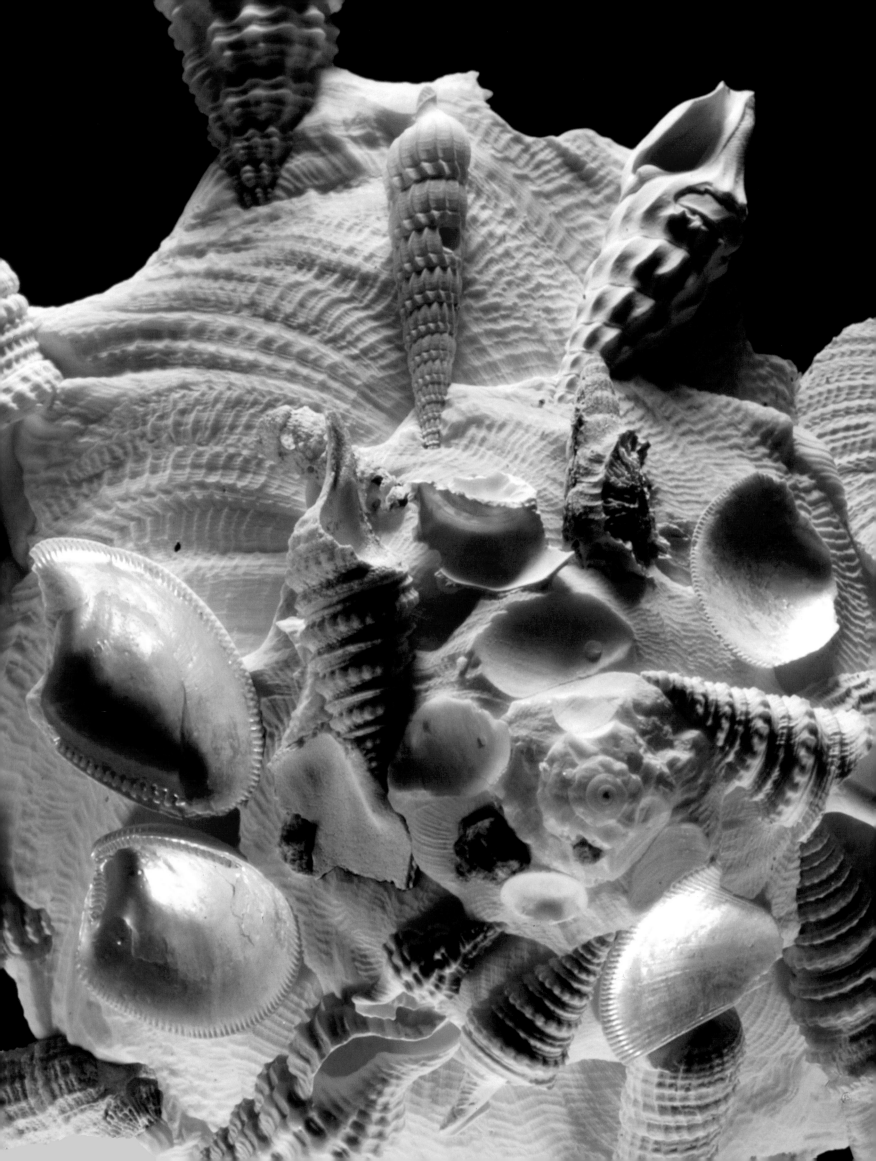

temperature, or the finding of a new hominid fossil in South America. Many results that are of interest to us zoologists or taxonomists would appear trivial to a physicist or a geneticist and do not fall within this range of "exceptional" results, so that type of paper would be mercilessly rejected by the top ranking journals.

Who decides what is good and can be published and what is less good—or of less interest—and should be rejected? Each scientific journal has an editor in chief who is a researcher in the field of knowledge covered by the publication in question. But no one is omniscient, and no editor in chief has the skills necessary to read, judge, and assess all the papers sent to his or her journal. The editor in chief therefore relies on a panel of referees. These are researchers working in the same field as the author of the paper and who are assumed to be *au fait* with the latest results, the most relevant methods of analysis, and, in general, the state of the art on the subject of the article or paper. In the case of a description of a new species, these are the people who will judge whether the characters have been properly analyzed, if the illustrations are adequate, and whether some obscure publication has escaped the attention of the author. The judges' assessment is often anonymous, so that they are able to tell some big shot that his work has been shoddy, or that the results are inconsistent; of course, in order to be credible and to be taken into account by the editor of the journal, the referees have to justify their opinions. It's not enough just to say, "It's no good"; they have to explain why. So in this great game of the publication of research results, everyone successively plays the part of the cop and the robber, the judge and the judged, the assessor and the assessed. This is what is known as "peer review."

Scientific journals are usually published quarterly and the series of events from submission of the paper, its arbitration and being returned to the author for corrections to the actual appearance of the paper in print can take an average of one year. From the "assumption of a discovery" on the deck of the ship, to the "confirmed discovery" in the laboratory of the specialist, then to the "sharing of the discovery" at the time of publication, taxonomic research thus takes place at a pace and timescale that is far longer than what the news media call "breaking news."

Pages 50–51, 53–55. As their name indicates, the xenophores (from the Greek xenos, "stranger," and pherein, "carry"), or carrier shells, attach the shells of other species to their own, as well as gravel and even manufactured materials such as shards of glass or coins. Most sought after by collectors are attachments of Coca-Cola bottle tops. Xenophora pallidula *(Reeve, 1842) (pages 50–51, and see also page 101; Philippines, 55 mm [2¼ in.]) is a true shell collector, while* Xenophora longleyi *(Bartsch, 1931) (pages 53–55; Gulf of Mexico, 140 mm [5½ in.]) has a less flamboyant, almost minimalist style.*

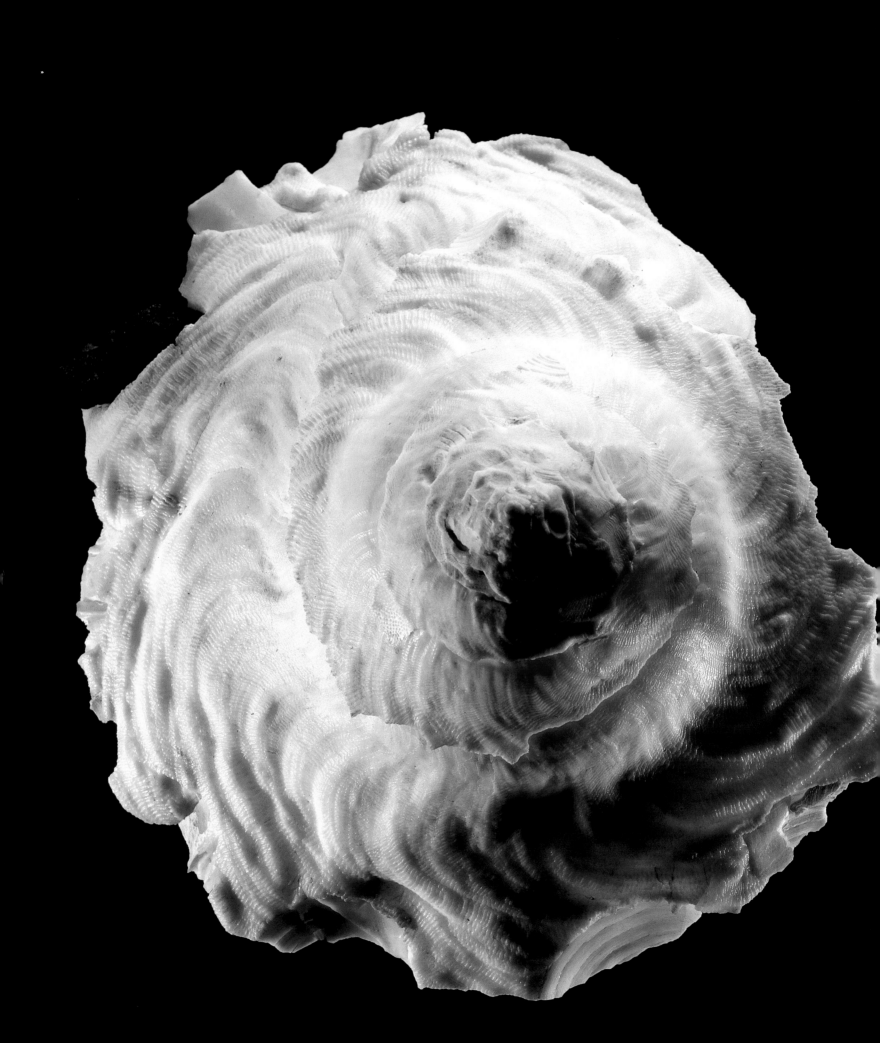

Naming Shells

Conus gauguini.
When Georges Richard and Bernard Salvat named this cone shell from the Marquesas in 1974, they chose to honor the painter Paul Gauguin, who had spent the last years of his life on these islands. His paintings symbolize the exoticism and languor of the Pacific. The violet background color of the shell is reminiscent of the artist's work. Marquesas, 72 mm (2¾ in.).

Imagine that I am interested in the reproductive behavior of the whelk in order to better evaluate the stocks of the species and help to manage them as a resource on the coasts of New England. So as not to reinvent the wheel and do the same research that has already been done in another country, or to compare my results with those obtained elsewhere, I need to consult the scientific publications on this subject. But I hit a snag. The species I call *whelk* in New England is called *buccin* in Canada, *bulot* in France, *Wellhornschnecke* in Germany, and *kongesnegl* in Norway. There is also the problem that the English word *whelk* is rather imprecise and can be used to designate any large spindle-shaped gastropod with a short siphonal canal. The "Common and Scientific Names of Mollusks" lists no less than 69 North American species that have *whelk* as part of their name. In fact, if a British or American researcher uses the word *whelk* to report the results of his studies, I cannot be really sure that they are talking about the same whelk that I am. And how will I know what they mean in Iceland by *Beitukóngur*? Very early on, scientists encountered the obstacle of the Tower of Babel when it came to the names of species. It was realized that each species needed to be designated, wherever it might be in the world, by a single valid name that would apply to it alone.

Although the days when scientists communicated with each other in Latin are long gone, the names of species remain in Latin. Such names consist of two words: the name of the genus, which starts with a capital or uppercase letter, and a specific epithet. which begins with a lowercase letter. This is known as the binominal or binomial nomenclature. In binominal nomenclature, what is known as a *bulot* on French fishmarkets, the *Wellhornschnecke* of the North Sea, is *Buccinum undatum*. The species was first given this name by Linnaeus in 1758, so Linnaeus is known as the author of the name. By extension, although incorrectly, he is said to be the author of the species. The author and date of the description do not form part of the name of the species, but it is common practice to give them after the scientific name to facilitate bibliographical research; so the full name of the waved whelk is *Buccinum undatum* Linnaeus, 1758, the Atlantic king scallop is *Pecten maximus* (Linnaeus, 1758), and the edible oyster is *Ostrea edulis* Linnaeus, 1758.

These three scientific names follow two of the rules of zoological nomenclature. The first rule is that there must be a grammatical gender agreement between the name of the genus and the specific epithet. In Latin, *Buccinum* is neuter, so the specific epithet, *undatus* (masculine), *undata* (feminine), and *undatum* (neuter), when combined with it must be in the neuter: *Buccinum undatum. Pecten* is masculine, so the specific epithet, *maximus, maxima, maximum*, must be combined with it in the masculine: *Pecten maximus. Ostrea* is feminine, so the specific epithet, *edulis, edulis, edule*, will be combined with it in the feminine: *Ostrea edulis.*

The second rule is more esoteric. You will note that the name Linnaeus, and the date, 1758, are in parentheses in the case of *Pecten maximus*, but there are no parentheses in the case of *Buccinum undatum* and *Ostrea edulis*. This convention is there to alert taxonomists to the fact that Linnaeus did not originally place the scallop in the genus *Pecten*. Linnaeus had very extensive concepts for the generic names he used. That is quite understandable in view of the very small number of species of which he was aware. It is as if one were in the situation of sorting tools and parts. If you are new to the hardware trade, a dozen drawers might be enough for you to arrange nails, screws, and screwdrivers; if, on the other hand, you are a major hardware store, you will need to be able to differentiate between round-headed screws, notched screws, steel nails, brass nails, and so on. In a way, it could be said that Linnaeus was a beginner at biodiversity inventory, since he only needed fifteen genera in which to classify all of the bivalves, whereas today, we need two thousand. Linnaeus classified the scallop in the genus *Ostrea*; when Otto Müller established the genus *Pecten* in 1776 and placed the scallop in it, the epithet was retained and *Ostrea maxima* Linnaeus, 1758 became *Pecten maximus* (Linnaeus, 1758).

Of course, these rules did not fall from the sky. They are embodied in the International Code of Zoological Nomenclature laid down by the International Commission on Zoological Nomenclature, whose

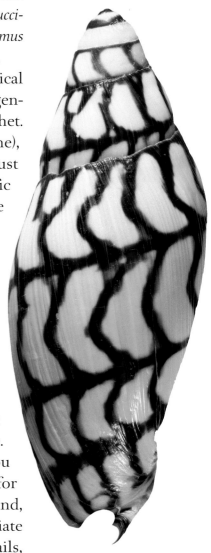

Another Australian specialty, the volutes, are nicknamed as a group "the Rolls-Royce of conchology." Volutes are eagerly collected because of their beauty. Many are rare and prized. Although Volutoconus bednalli *(Brazier, 1878) is today affordable for most beginning collectors, for years it fetched record prices at shell auctions. Australia, Northern Territory, 107 mm (4¼ in.).*

headquarters are in London at the Natural History Museum. The commission, which is itself under the authority of the International Union of Biological Sciences, consists of twenty-eight members, who represent all of the branches of zoology and paleozoology. The same rules are actually applied to animals of every shape and size, past and present, from mosquitoes to dinosaurs, from amoebas to monkeys, from squids to sparrows. In addition to representing the various branches of zoology, the international twenty-eight member commission also needs to encompass the various scientific communities or schools of thought. For a long time, the International Commission on Zoological Nomenclature was very much a club of European or North American men. Today, it also includes Chinese, Latin Americans, and since 2006, women. I have been a member of the august commission since 1991, and my colleague Gary Rosenberg, from the Academy of Natural Sciences of Philadelphia, and I are the only two malacologists currently serving on it. The commission operates almost exclusively by e-mail; in fact, since I have been a member, it has only physically met a couple of times, including a week-long meeting in Budapest, in the summer of 1995, to prepare the fourth edition of the famous International Code of Zoological Nomenclature.

As a commission member, I would be untruthful if I told you that I don't enjoy mulling over or discussing a nomenclature problem with a colleague, but after two or three hours, I start to tire of it and would like to move on to something else. The prospect of devoting a whole week of my summer exclusively to zoological nomenclature originally looked to me like a form of punishment, freely agreed to, of course, but punishment nevertheless. In fact, I have wonderful memories—almost exalted ones—of that week of discussions, during which technical arguments were scrutinized, and generous and farsighted objectives and ideals were challenged by the realities of how taxonomists practice their science. The devil very much hides in the details, and with millions of names established by generations of zoologists, a forest of details can defeat the application of the best of principles. This is why the Code of Nomenclature appears intimidating and impenetrable to a beginner. The International Commission on Zoological Nomenclature has only its own moral authority with which to impose its regulations: it has no police force to issue tickets to violators, no fines to impose, no taxonomic jail or penitentiary for lawbreakers. The system works because everyone—or almost everyone—agrees that there have

▷▷
Pages 60–61.
Contrary to the belief of certain collectors, Thatcheria mirabilis *was not named in homage to Margaret Thatcher, who was not even born when George French Angas gave it its name in 1877, but in honor of a certain Charles Thatcher whom history has forgotten. Originally known only from a single specimen, it was thought by many to be a freak, and Angas was derided for giving it a name.*
Pacific Ocean, 71 mm (2¾ in.).

NAMING SHELLS

to be rules and they follow them. So the rules need to be logical and commonsensical, without giving the impression that they favor one school of thought over another, or one country over another. During the period of discussions about the code, some zoologists suggested that descriptions of new species ought in future to be published in a language that uses the Latin alphabet. In other words, in future, descriptions would not be permitted in Korean, Armenian, or Arabic (in practice there are very few of these, but there are some, mainly on insects or fossils). Well, if a consensus might perhaps be reached about such a rule, it would permit Croatian (which is written in Latin characters) to be used but not Serbian (which uses the Cyrillic alphabet, like Russian), even though they are basically the same language; Hungarian and Lithuanian (which are spoken by only a few million people) could be used, but Russian, Japanese, and Chinese would be banned. That is obviously ridiculous, and the proposal was swiftly thrown out. I believe that, ideally, all the descriptions should appear in the same language, and I suggested that the language in question could be none other than English. But we don't live in an ideal world, and English is perceived by many people as a vehicle for linguistic, cultural, and political imperialism, so my counterproposal was also rejected. We don't live in a world that places science on one side and politics or culture on the other side, and this includes the International Commission on Zoological Nomenclature.

Taxonomists are granted an exceptional privilege. Whenever they describe a new species, it is entirely up to them to choose the scientific name by which it will be known. They have almost total freedom of choice for that name. In the eighteenth and nineteenth centuries, zoologists, who were then thoroughly steeped in classical culture, used such names as those of the Muses or the Olympian gods and goddesses. That is why Linnaeus himself used the name of Clio (the Muse of history) for a planktonic pteropod; Antoine Risso used Erato (the Muse of lyric and love poetry) for a Mediterranean gastropod; Poli applied the name of Artemis (the goddess of hunting and nature) to a bivalve, and Denys de Montfort that of Apollo (the god of beauty, of course) to a tropical gastropod. But there were only nine Muses and only twelve Olympian gods, so this source of names soon ran out. With the nymphs, of whom there were three thousand just among the Oceanids, there were still plenty to choose from. This resulted in

▷
Earlier authors gave these shells of the family Architectonicidae the common name of "sundials." In these days of digital watches the name has (unfortunately?) fallen into disuse. The Latin name, Architectonica perspectiva *(Linnaeus, 1758), is universal and timeless, however. Indian and Pacific oceans, 39 mm (1¾ in.).*

Hyalaea Lamarck, 1799 (a pteropod), *Halia* Risso, 1826 (a volute), *Potamides* Brongniart, 1810 (a fossil from the Paris Basin and a snail from mangrove swamps), *Neaera* Gray, 1834 (a bivalve), and many more. Today, few taxonomists have been raised on Aristotle or Pliny, and the Code of Nomenclature permits any name that is "Latin, derived from Latin, Greek or any other language, or formed from such a word," and even "an arbitrary combination of letters, providing this is formed to be used as a word." Now that they are not restricted to the classical dictionaries, malacologists have let their imaginations run wild, from *Allo allo* Jousseaume, 1934, to *Abra cadabra* Eames & Wilkins, 1957. Even acronyms can be latinized. A few years ago, I actually named a gastropod living around the deep-sea hot vents near the islands of Fiji *Ifremeria nautilei*. I chose the genus name *Ifremeria* in homage to the role of Ifremer, the *Institut français de recherche pour l'exploitation de la mer*, which has been—and remains—one of the global players in exploration of the deep ocean; the specific epithet *nautilei* (the genitive of *nautileus*, the latinization of "Nautile") is a reminder of the research submersible Le *Nautile*, which enabled the discovery and exploration of these hydrothermal vents. So "dog Latin," as it is sometimes known, is very much part of zoological nomenclature.

Opposite and above. As an example of a blunder sanctioned by the Code of Nomenclature, Linnaeus thought that Trochus niloticus, *a topshell or topsnail, lived in the Nile, hence the name he gave to the species. The Code does not require names to be appropriate or relevant, and* niloticus *has remained the name of this species even though it is now known that it lives on coral platforms in the Indian and Pacific oceans. After all, as Shakespeare said, "What's in a name? that which we call a rose/By any other name would smell as sweet."*

Is it a throwback to the time when the names of new creatures were dedicated to the Muses or the Greco-Roman gods if taxonomists like to use their creative freedom to pay homage to their colleagues, to their nearest and dearest, to sponsors, philanthropists, or even to celebrities? Thus, the gastropod *Cymbiola rossiniana* (Bernardi, 1859) was named in homage to the famous composer, Gioacchino Rossini, who was a contemporary of Bernardi. *Fusus grimaldii* Dautzenberg & Fischer, 1896 is named for Prince Albert I of Monaco, of the House of Grimaldi, a famous marine biologist who surveyed the deep sea fauna of the North Atlantic on his yachts *Hirondelle* and *Princesse Alice*. The specific epithet of the name *Pyrunculus fourierii* (Audouin, 1826) honors the memory of Joseph Fourier, the brilliant mathematician, discoverer of the trigonometic series known as Fourier analysis. A strong supporter of the French Revolution, Fourier was the recruiter for the *Commission des sciences et des arts* [Committee for Science and Arts], which discovered this tiny species of gastropod in the Red Sea in the course of Napoleon Bonaparte's Egyptian campaign. Contrary to the belief of many collectors, *Thatcheria mirabilis* is not named in homage to Margaret Thatcher, who was not even born in 1877 when George French Angas established the name, but after a certain Charles Thatcher whom history has forgotten. On the other hand, Emperor Hirohito of Japan was the subject of the dedication of *Rotaovula hirohitoi* Cate & Azuma, 1973; the name has made this small ovulid species from the seas around southern Japan and the Philippines particularly sought after by Japanese collectors. I myself have given in—without abusing the privilege so I can maintain

Page 69.
The Isle of Pines volute Cymbiola rossiniana *(Bernardi, 1859) lives only off the southern tip of New Caledonia, at a depth of a few to a few dozen meters (10 to 200 feet). The volute's nocturnal habits afford it some protection against excessive collecting, but its restricted distribution and its large size cause this species to be particularly vulnerable. It may become necessary to regulate the collection and trade in this shell. New Caledonia, 155 mm (6¼ in.).*

Left and pages 66–67.
To most of us, the pattern on the valves of Lioconcha castrensis *(Linnaeus, 1758) is evocative of mountains in a Chinese painting. For Linnaeus, they looked like the tents of a military encampment—the "cas-trum" of Roman writers—hence the specific name he gave it. Indian and Pacific oceans, 48 mm (1¾ in.).*

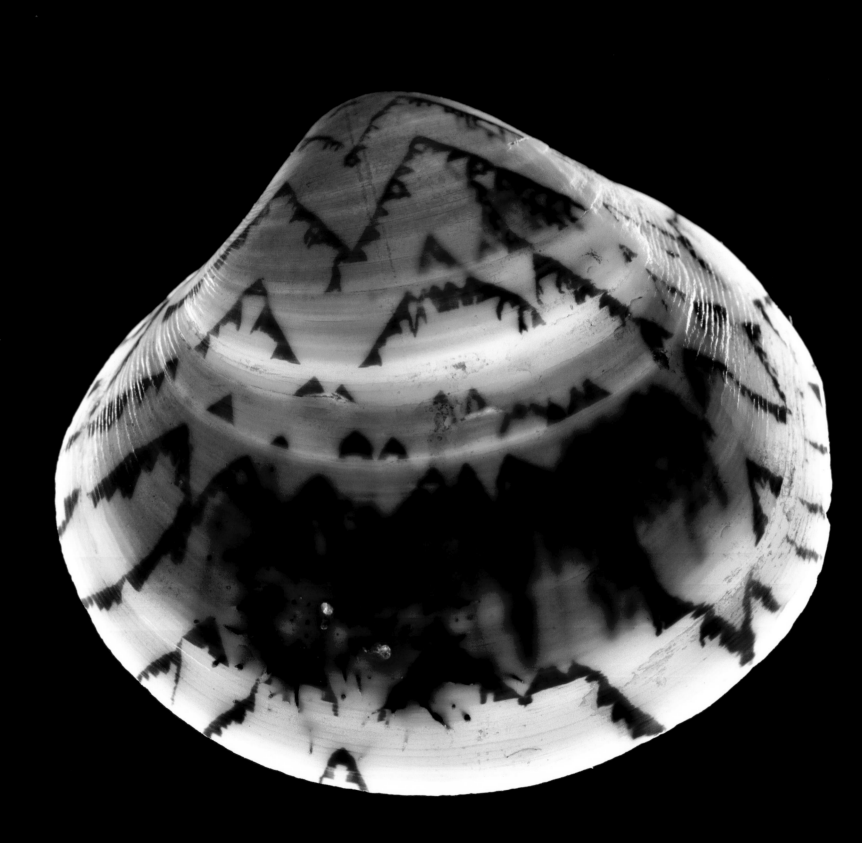

the value of such gestures—to this practice of dedicating new species to individuals. Sometimes they are not even real people, as when my colleague Anders Warén of the Stockholm Museum and I assigned the name *Marginella aronnax*. Professor Aronnax is a character in *Twenty Thousand Leagues Under the Sea*. During the voyages of the *Nautilus*, Jules Verne stopped his submarine off the coast of Papua next to the island of Geboroar; Aronnax and his servant, Counsel, go onshore to hunt for shells and discover a sinistral olive shell that delights the professor—until a spiteful native smashes it with an adroitly aimed rock. But there have also been real people involved, such as when, at my request, Emilio Garcia dedicated *Cycloscala sardellae* Garcia, 2004, to Gina Sardella-Sadiki, assistant to the program director of the Total Foundation, which made possible the Lifou 2000 Expedition, during the course of which this species was discovered.

More commonly, the names of species are a reminder of a morphological peculiarity, the geographical location in which they were discovered, or a feature of their behavior. *Coralliophila violacea* (Kiener, 1836) is a gastropod that lives on corals and at their expense (*corallium*, "coral" and *philein*, "to love"), and this species has a violet-colored mouth. *Pisolamia brychia* (Watson, 1883) and *Megadenus oneirophantae* Bouchet & Lützen, 1980 are two parasitic gastropods that live on a deep-sea holothurian; the genus name *Pisolamia* is formed from *pisum*, "pea," and *lamia*, "vampire," in reference to their parasitical lifestyle and the spherical shape of their shells; *brychia* comes from the Greek to express the fact that this species lives at great depths; the specific epithet *oneirophantae* indicates that the snail is parasitic on the holothurian *Oneirophanta mutabilis*. In the case of *Zygoceras tropidophora* Warén & Bouchet, 1991, the genus name is a reminder that it is similar and related to (from the Greek *zygos*, "pair") *Haloceras*, and the specific epithet alludes to the shell being keeled (like the hull of a boat) in shape (from the Greek *tropis* or *tropidos*, "keel," and *pherein*, "to

◁

Lioconcha castrensis
(see also page 68, bottom).
This edible bivalve belongs to the family Veneridae, which on our shores includes hard-shelled clams as the quahog.
Indian and Pacific oceans, 48 mm (1¾ in.).

▷

In the case of Turbo petholatus *Linnaeus, 1758, (above right) it is hard to know which to admire most, the shell or the operculum. The calcareous operculum of the Turbinidae or turban shells is used in costume jewelry and even, in the case of the larger species, as a paperweight. The color of this operculum, white on the periphery and blue-green in the center, has given it the name of "cat's-eye," although older sources refer to the shell as "tapestry turbo."*
Pacific Ocean, 50 mm (2 in.).

71

NAMING SHELLS

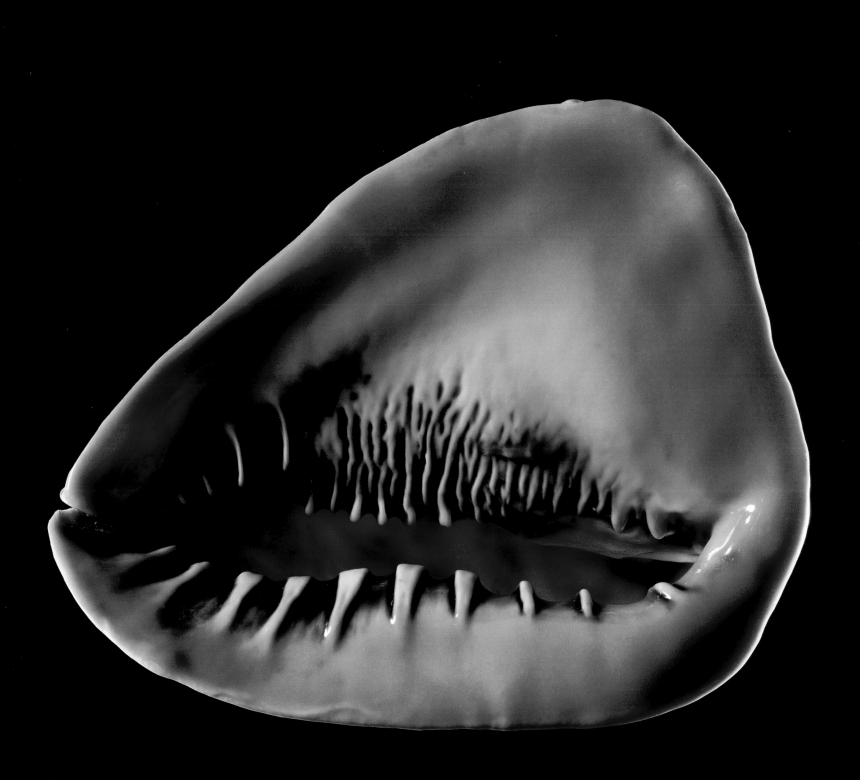

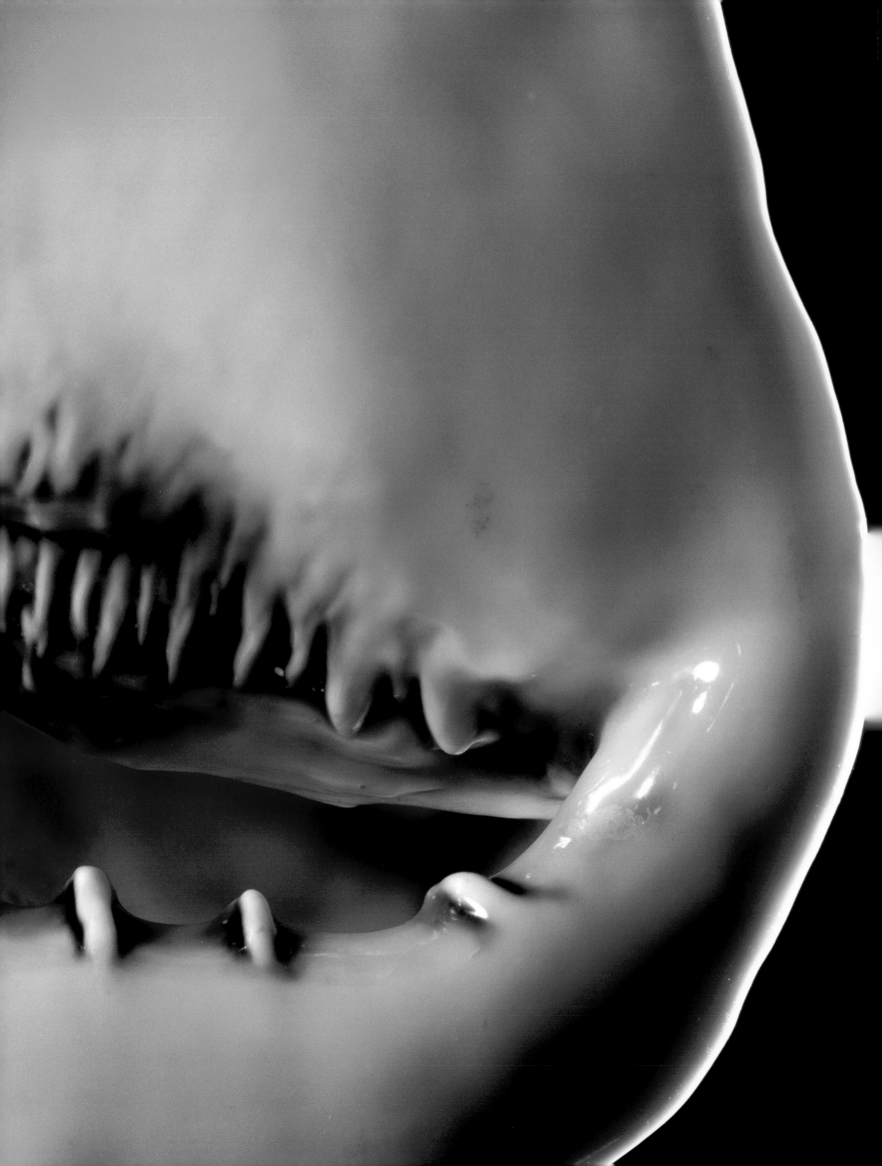

Pages 72–74.

The scientific name of the emperor or queen helmet also results from a blunder: contrary to what its name might suggest, Cassis madagascariensis *Lamarck, 1822 does not live in the Indian Ocean, but in the Caribbean. A genuinely Madagascan helmet shell,* Cypraecassis rufa *(Linnaeus, 1758), is used as a raw material on which to carve cameos. Could this have been the source of Lamarck's confusion?*

Pages 76–77.

Unlike Trochus niloticus *and* Cassis madagascariensis, *names may be descriptive and evocative, such as that of this* Venus foliaceolamellosus *Dillwyn, 1817, whose specific epithet is particularly appropriate. Senegal, 80 mm (3¼ in.).*

bear or carry"). *Amaea guineensis* Bouchet & Tillier, 1978 comes from the Gulf of Guinea, and *Amalda bellonarum* Kilburn & Bouchet, 1988 was discovered around the Bellona Islands in the Coral Sea. As for *Eccliseogyra exquisita* Bouchet & Warén, 1986 and *Buccinaria pygmaea* Bouchet & Sysoev, 1997, their specific epithets speak for themselves.

To date a million and a half species of animals are known, as well as several hundred thousand fossil species. Since Linnaeus's time, millions of names have been proposed, not always wisely and not always with the scientific rigor one would wish for today. Ensuring that each species is designated by a single name and that each name is used for a single species is not as trivial a matter as one might think. In fact, it is not unusual for the same species to have been named several times. There are many reasons for this. The two commonest reasons are the involuntary ignorance of works already published, on the one hand, and insufficient understanding of the variability of an already described species, on the other. As an example of the former, when the Japanese malacologist Tadashige Habe described a volute found in the Philippines in 1975 as *Lyria kawamurai*, he was unaware that the same species had been described by Harry Ladd, an American paleontologist, a few months earlier from the island of Espiritu Santo, in the New Hebrides (now known as Vanuatu), under the name of *Lyria santoensis* Ladd, 1975. Years went by, and eventually it was realized that as early as 1903, George Sowerby III had called this same seashell *Voluta planicostata*. As an example of the latter, in 1985, the Spanish malacologist Emilio Rolán discovered at a depth of about fifteen meters (50 feet) in the Ria de Vigo a colony of gastropods of the Muricidae family with an imbricated sculpture that looked like nothing known in the region. The species was described as a new one under the name *Coralliophila rolani* Bogi & Nofroni, 1984 in homage to its discoverer. When the description was published, I realized immediately that this was the small dog-whelk known as *Nucella lapillus*, a very common species on the European Atlantic coasts. The marine biologist Louis Cabioch from the Marine Biological Station in Roscoff, in Brittany, had shown me some very similar specimens with an imbricated sculpture, which he had dredged up from the English Channel off Cape Blanchart. *Nucella lapillus* is normally a species that is strictly confined to the intertidal zone; however, in areas swiped by strong currents, it may live exceptionally down to a depth of twenty meters (65 feet), although

such specimens are smaller, with more fragile and imbricated shells, which at first glance make them appear very unlike specimens that live in tidal areas. Hence the confusion of the European researchers. So what happens in such a case? The Code of Nomenclature edicts a "Principle of Priority" whereby when several names have been given to the same species, the oldest is the valid one, the rest being treated as synonyms. In the examples quoted, the valid name of the volute is *Lyria planicostata* (Sowerby, 1903), and *Lyria kawamurai* Habe 1975 and *Lyria santoensis* Ladd, 1975 are synonyms; *Nucella lapillus* (Linnaeus, 1758) is the valid name, and *Coralliophila rolani* Bogi & Nofroni, 1984 is a synonym.

The Code has another guiding principle, the "Principle of Homonymy." This means that two animal species, whatever they may be, cannot bear the same name. When, in 1878, the Norwegian zoologist G. O. Sars described the gastropod *Lovenella metula*, in honor of the Swede Sven Lovén, he was not aware that the name *Lovenella* had already been used in 1869 by Hincks for a hydroid. Could a hydroid be confused with a gastropod? Of course not. But the principle of homonymy cannot be applied selectively. A land snail and a sea snail cannot be given the same name, nor can a gazelle and a squirrel, or a mosquito and a bird. By virtue of the principle of priority, the most recently published name must give way and be replaced. In 1882, the American malacologist A. H. Verrill suggested the name of *Cerithiella* as a replacement for *Lovenella*, and the gastropod described by Sars is currently known by the name of *Cerithiella metula* (G. O. Sars, 1878). The principle of homonymy also applies to specific epithets if these are combined with the same genus name. *Alvania lactea* (Michaud, 1830) and *Striarca lactea* (Linnaeus, 1758) are not homonyms, but *Cerithium lacteum* Philippi, 1836 and *Cerithium lacteum* Kiener, 1841 are; the most recent name must give way and *Cerithium lacteum* Kiener, 1841 is known today as *Cerithium nesioticum* Pilsbry & Vanatta, 1906.

Despite these simple and commonsensical rules—and there are many more that it would not be appropriate to discuss here—nomenclature is denounced by some biologists as being a source of outdated or even unscientific restrictions. It is easy to poke fun at the fact that all the names are in Latin—in an age when hardly anyone knows that language—or to complain about the principle of priority as a source of instability and one that favors mediocrity. Admittedly, the application of this principle can indeed lead to a name published with a good description being replaced by an older synonym originally published with a mediocre description. This is what caused the great evolutionist and essayist Stephen J. Gould to remark: "In fields other than science, the work of incompetents is ignored; in taxonomy, due to the principle of priority, their work is protected." In fact, some well-intentioned minds have proposed changing to a digital system of nomenclature, which would be more stable while retaining the same precision. However, it isn't hard to understand why such a system has never caught on. Take common events in a day. We say hello to Hugo Plumel, and we lunch with Erika Strong; we don't say hello to 425-45-0576, and we don't lunch with 020-91-2299. Names do not just perform the function of designation in electronic databases, they also have the function of communication between men and women. In this respect, memorable, pronounceable names that are etymologically significant are much more appropriate than series of figures. After all, in most societies, individuals are designated by a family name and a first name, and this approach is paralleled in the scientific names of species, which also consist of the name of a genus and a specific epithet. If Linnaeus's binomial nomenclature has remained universally accepted for more than two hundred fifty years, it is because it intuitively corresponds to our social model of designating living organisms.

Pages 78–79.
Shells preserved by scientists in museum collections are generally in their "natural" state, i.e., untreated and even uncleaned. Collectors, however, remove any unattractive incrustation and bring up the brilliance of the colors by coating shells in paraffin wax. In the Philippines, in the case of rare—and expensive—species, some dealers even repair damaged spines or lips, or plug holes in the shell. Shells treated in this way may be hard to recognize in relation to what can be seen in the wild. Page 78, Morula musiva *(Kiener, 1836), Pacific Ocean, 22 mm (1 in.); page 79,* Pirenella conica *(Blainville, 1826), Tunisia,15 mm (⅝ in.)*

Pages 80–81.
Hexaplex regius *(Swainson, 1821) belongs to the same family as* Bolinus brandaris *(Linnaeus, 1758) and* Trunculariopsis trunculus *(Linnaeus, 1758), which live in the Mediterranean and from which the ancients made Tyrrhian purple. The Native Americans of* the Pacific Coast independently discovered this secretion by murex shells. Hexaplex regius *is not common enough there, however, to give rise to such a craft, and in the pre-Columbian era, the local people used* Plicopurpura pansa *(Gould, 1853) to make a purple dye.*
Peru, 125 mm (4½ in.).

The Role of Natural History Museums

Pages 82, 84, 86–87.
Although brightly colored and spiny, Ctenocardia victor *(Angas, 1872), opposite, has an undeniable family resemblance to the humble cockle shell (family Cardiidae) living on our coasts. Similarly,* Bassina disjecta *(Perry, 1811) (pages 84, 86–87) has an air of family with the hard-shelled clams and is classified with them in the family Veneridae. Other classifications are more unexpected. For instance, scientists have recently discovered that the giant clams actually belong to the Cardiidae and do not form a separate family as they had believed for two centuries. C. victor: Philippines. Size: 47 mm (1¾ in.); B. disjecta: Australia, 45 mm (1¾ in.).*

When taxonomists describe a new species of plant or animal, they give it a name and describe it as completely as possible. But of course, they can only do so with the technological tools available to them at the time and in reference to what was known in the past. I myself began my professional career at the time of the advent of the scanning electron microscope, a tool that has revolutionized the observation—and illustration—of the most minute details of the sculpture of shells. A description considered to be adequate at one moment in the history of zoology may subsequently be judged superficial and inadequate twenty or a hundred years later. Thus, the descriptions by Linnaeus or Lamarck, which at the time were considered with respect by other zoologists, are nowadays judged to be quite inadequate for characterizing the species they named. Who recognizes today, in the elliptical phrase "*Buccinum testa ovata: striis transversis elevatis glabris, ventro obtuse quinqangulari, labro intus striato*" (A whelk with an ovate shell, with smooth, raised transverse striations, a body with five obtuse whorls, and a lip striated on the inside), the whelk *Buccinum undatum*, which I have used as my demonstration model in these essays? Such a description could apply to dozens, or even hundreds of species. At the time when Linnaeus was writing his *Systema Naturae*, the northern Pacific had barely been mapped, and of course, he was unaware that the scientific exploration of Japan, the Sea of Okhotsk, and the seas around Alaska would lead to the discovery of many other species of *Buccinum* to which his description for *Buccinum undatum* would be applicable. So what should be done? Should the name *Buccinum undatum* be abandoned? Why not? But that would be as if it were decided to abandon the word *copper* or *lead*, just because the definitions given to them by metallurgists in antiquity or chemists working at the time of the Thirteen Colonies are outdated and no longer represent what we know about the atomic structure of these metals. To take the comparison a little further, should a name be changed each time an important feature is discovered that had previously gone unnoticed and that therefore had not been included in the description? Should we change the name if we discover an inaccuracy or an error in the description? The risks of instability and absurdity inherent in such proposals are immeasurable. The fact that twenty-first-century malacologists no longer define *Buccinum undatum* using the same words and the same features as Linnaeus is quite normal and reflects the progress of knowledge, just as twenty-first-century chemists no longer describe copper or lead with the same words and the same features used by Antoine Lavoisier.

What enables taxonomists to stabilize the usage of the scientific names they employ is the link between the name and a specimen used for reference, which is known as the *name-bearing type*. Thus, whatever the state of our knowledge, what defines the name *Buccinum undatum* is not the description given to it by Linnaeus, but the name-bearing type with which Linnaeus associated that name. Name-bearing types constitute the reference standards for zoological and botanical nomenclature. Obviously, they are unique for each name. *Buccinum undatum* may well have a geographical distribution that extends from Russia to Canada, via Norway, the North Sea, the British Isles, the French Atlantic coast, Iceland, and Greenland, but these countries do not have their "own" type of *Buccinum undatum*. This species has a single type which is preserved in the collection of the Linnean Society of London, at the headquarters of the society in Piccadilly. Researchers in any country have access to it and can examine it, checking on the state of a particular feature of the specimen that Linnaeus did not consider worth describing. This means that such types constitute prestigious heritage collections for museums. At the same time, they create obligations: the obligation of preservation and maintenance and the obligation of making the collection available to the international scientific community. Even during the tensest moments of the Cold War,

Page 85.
Trigonia, *so abundant in the seas of the Jurassic Period, became extinct in most of the world at the same time as the dinosaurs in the Late Cretaceous. The only survivors today are half a dozen species in the seas around Australia. This one is* Neotrigonia margaritacea *(Lamarck, 1804).*
Australia, 30 mm (1¼ in.).

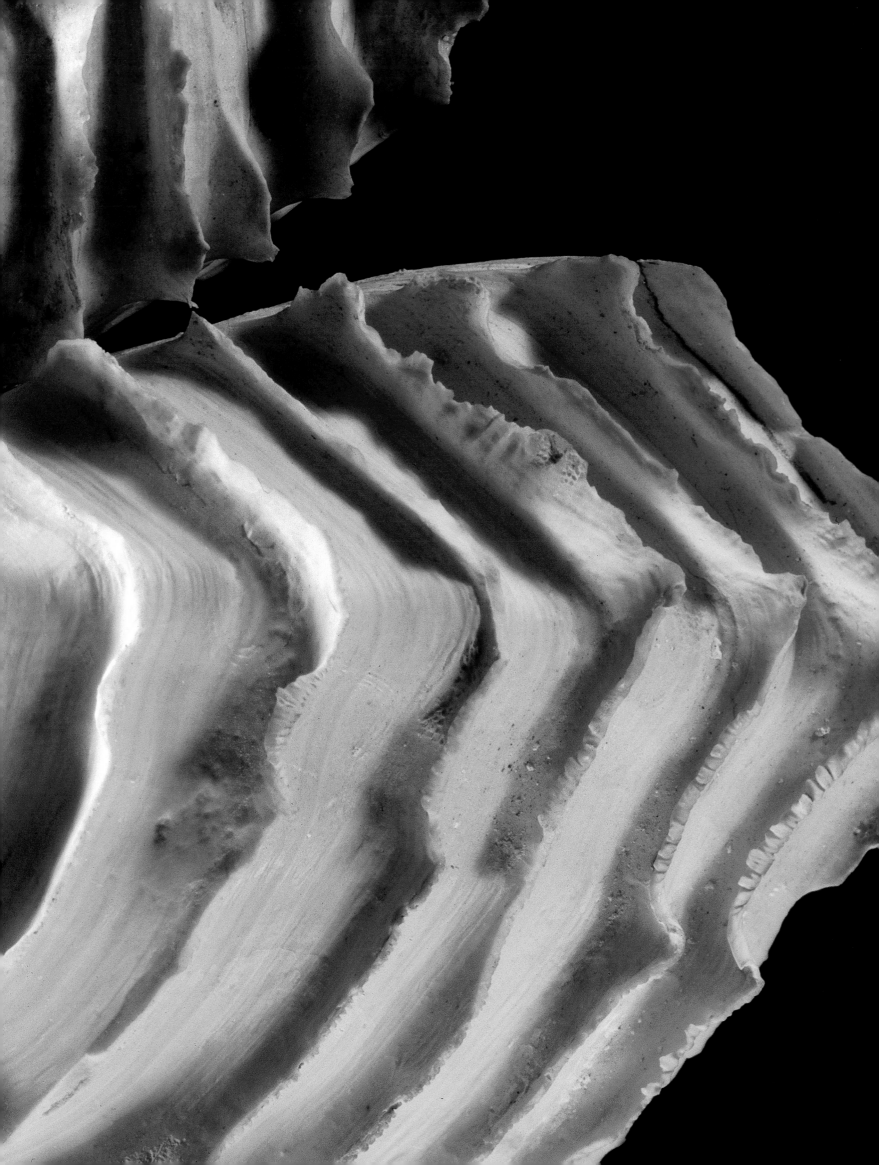

Pages 88–90.
The English conchologist Lowell Reeve named this shell from Palawan in the Philippines Delphinula melanacantha *(meaning "with black spines"). Some time later, the genus* Delphinula Lamarck, 1804 *was reclassified as a synonym of* Angaria Röding, 1798 *by virtue of the priority of date of publication. Today, this species is known by the name of* Angaria melanacantha *(Reeve, 1842). The parentheses around Reeve indicate the species is now in a genus that is different from the original one he used. Philippines, 30 mm (1¼ in.).*

Soviet researchers could consult the types at the National Museum of Natural History in Washington D.C., and American researchers could examine types in the Zoological Institute of the USSR Academy of Sciences in Leningrad. The use of the word *type* is one that has been consecrated by time, but the term is not devoid of ambiguity. A type is not a "typical" example of the species. In any case, what would a "typical" specimen be? A male or female? A specimen with the most common color pattern in the species? In fact, it doesn't matter. The type is nothing but the name-bearer or *onomatophore*. It is the interface between the virtual world of names and the real world of living organisms.

The very considerable scientific value of these types explains my tenacity in tracking down certain ones that were on the verge of disappearing and bringing them to the security of the collections of the Muséum national d'histoire naturelle. In the late 1970s, I accidentally discovered that someone called Edmond Saurin had published four articles between 1958 and 1962 on the Pyramidellidae (a family of microgastropods that parasitize other marine invertebrates) of Vietnam in the *Annales de la Faculté des Sciences de Saigon* [Annals of the Faculty of Science of Saigon]. I use the word "discover" because this is a fairly obscure publication. Despite Vietnam then being closely linked to France, the main library of my museum does not even own a complete set, and at the time, the work of Edmond Saurin had never been quoted by anyone else. Yet in these four articles Saurin described a treasure trove of 210 new species of Pyramidellidae, collected from among shell sand on the beaches of Vietnam. But where were the types? It was a mystery. I tried to find this Saurin, who apparently never maintained a link with any museum. I said to myself that even if he had returned from Vietnam in the early 1960s with only one suitcase, Pyramidellidae do not take up much room and, if I had been him, I would have brought back "my" types. My first move was to discuss the matter with Raoul Serène, a veteran carcinologist (a carcinologist is a specialist in crabs) who spent his whole career in Southeast Asia and who, at the time of my investigation, was working as an emeritus in the division of crustaceans at my museum.

By a chance in a thousand, Serène had actually met Edmond Saurin, and had visited him a few years previously where he was living near Aix-en-Provence, but he did not remember the address and considered himself to be too old (he was over eighty at the time) to go there with me. However, he put me in touch with a university lecturer in Lyon who had worked with him on the geological map of Indochina; this man in turn sent me to the Bureau of Geological and Mining Research, whose human resources department in Orléans, France, eventually found an address for me—one that was fifteen years old. I thus wrote to Saurin at the Château du Roussier, asking him whether by chance he had kept the pyramidellid types he had described and whether he would agree to deposit them at the museum. Two weeks later the reply came—from his widow. Edmond Saurin had died two years earlier, and Madame Saurin had no idea whether the samples I was seeking still existed, but the attic of their house was full of crates and boxes, and

I was welcome to come and see her. Two months later, accompanied by Annie, a museum technician, I was at the Château du Roussier. We were met by a charming elderly lady who, over a glass of port, told us about the couple's first trip to Indochina in 1937. They first sailed to Port Said, crossed the Red Sea in the company of the notorious French adventurer and arms smuggler, Henry de Monfreid (I'm not making this up), then on to Colombo and Hanoi. Her husband wanted to study the geology of Yunnan province but could not get visas and permits from the Chinese authorities so he "fell back" on Indochina [the old name for Vietnam, Laos and Cambodia, then French colonies], which he covered for twenty-five years. Saurin "discovered" the world of microshells around the 1950s, and so it was at that time that he briefly became enthusiastic about the Pyramidellidae, an interlude in the life of a scientist and eclectic collector. "But I'm just chatting and chatting," said Madame Saurin, "and you want to see the crates; we'll have to go up to the attic before it gets dark." A few minutes later, Annie and I found ourselves in a massive attic that covered a whole floor of the huge building, which looked something like Aladdin's cave. Annie and I looked at each other. It would take days and days to open all of these tin trunks, chests, and boxes. Looking for the pyramidellid types in all this would be like looking for a needle in a haystack. So what were we to do, now that we were so close to our goal? We told ourselves that, as the Pyramidellidae are so tiny, they ought logically to be inside small glass tubes. Knowing a common habit of old-timer collectors, these tubes would almost certainly be assembled in little boxes, probably cigar boxes. After a few minutes, we found the part of the attic containing collections of natural history items. There were rocks, fossils—and shells. By systematically searching chests containing the smallest drawers, we discovered the cigar boxes for which we had been looking. Finally, in less than fifteen minutes, we had put

△▷
Entemnotrochus adansonia-nus (Crosse & Fischer, 1861). When, in 1858, the fishermen of Marie-Galante, in Guadeloupe, brought the first specimen of this snail out of their lobster pots, they thought it was damaged, which would reduce its market value. So the shell (above) was "repaired" by filing the lip, then sold. In Paris, Hippolyte Crosse and Paul Fischer were not fooled and realized that this was a slit shell, a group of gastropods hitherto known only in the fossil state. The slit was there in nature, and the discovery was a scientific sensation. Guadeloupe (above) and Bahamas (right), 115 mm (4½ in.).

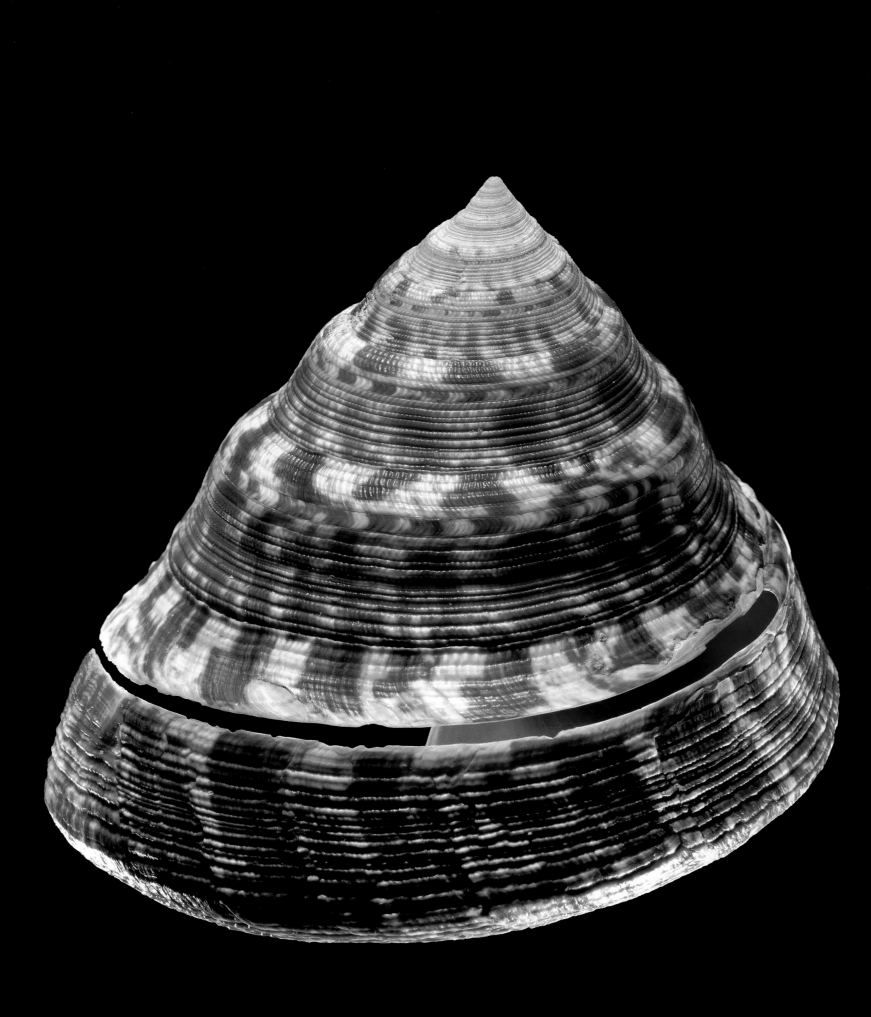

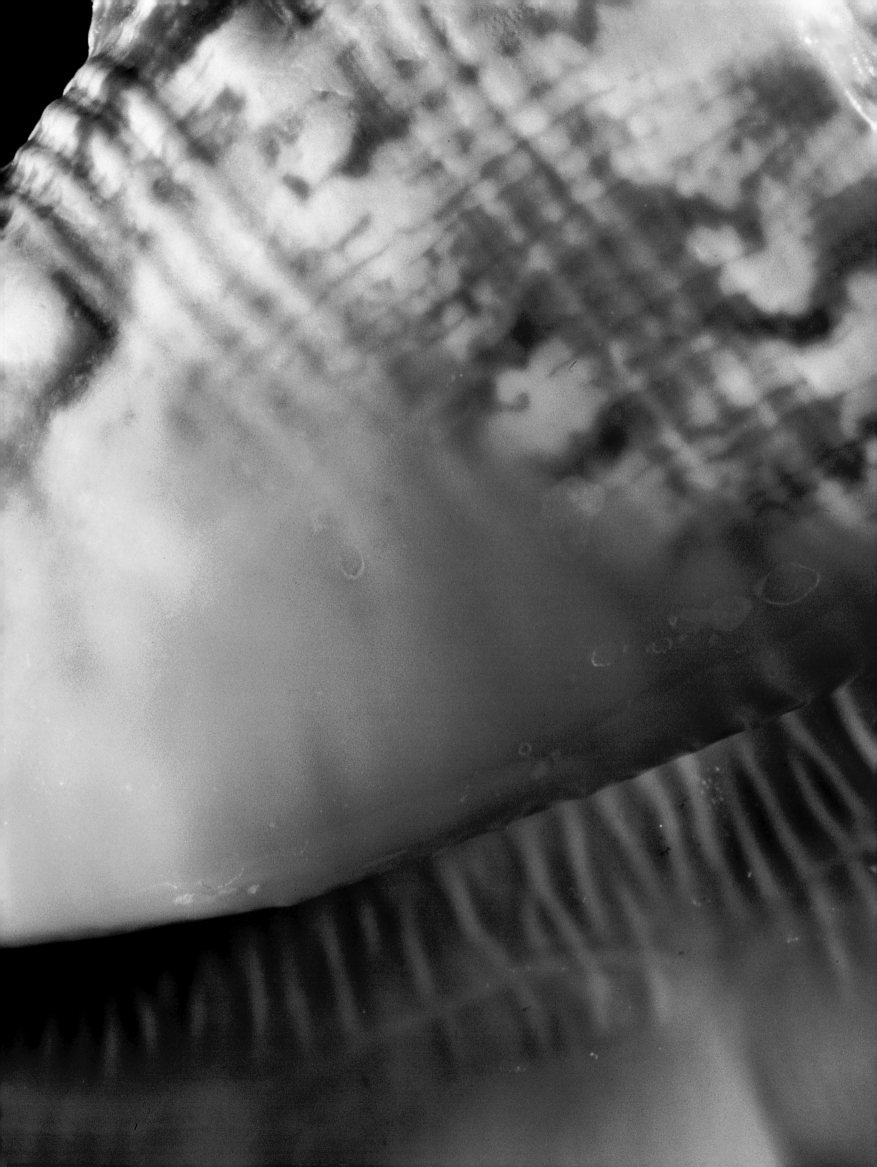

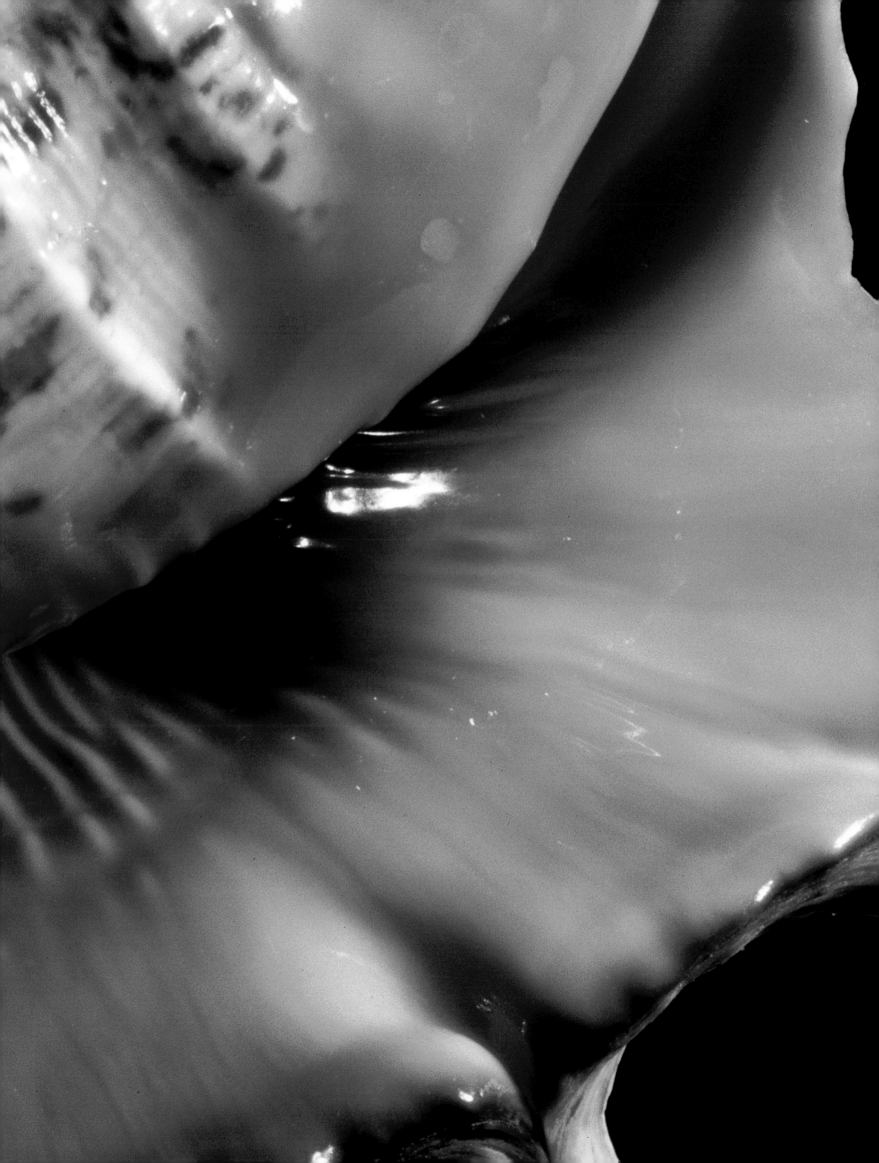

our hands on the Pyramidellidae from Vietnam. Victory! Madame Saurin gave us her blessing to take everything away, because in addition to the types we had been seeking, there were terrestrial mollusks wrapped in pieces of newspaper and others in a magnificent series of 1950s Indochinese matchboxes. On our return to the museum, Annie unpacked our treasure. Of the 210 species described by Saurin, we found more than 180 types, which are now housed in the museum's type collection. The fewer than thirty that are missing should be considered lost. They were species that had been packed in glass tubes that no longer had corks or species whose tubes were completely absent. Twenty-five years later, the tale of the Pyramidellidae in the Saurin collection remains one of the great hits of my career as a curator of the museum's collections.

Tenacity as well as sacrifice and ingenuity are needed in this field. Those responsible for the major collections always made arrangements for their charges to survive wars and revolutions. The collections of the Frankfurt Museum in Germany were housed at the end of World War II in a salt mine. Of course, there were losses, and the world's great conflicts have left scars in the zoological nomenclature. For instance, World War I is responsible for the destruction of the museum in Douai, in northern France, and, with it, the mollusk types described by Valéry-Louis Potiez and Gaspard Michaud in their *Galerie des mollusques, ou Catalogue méthodique, descriptif et raisonné des mollusques et coquilles du muséum de Douai* [Methodical, descriptive, and reasoned catalogue of the mollusks and shells in the Douai museum], published in installments between 1838 and 1844. Among the collateral damage caused by the Normandy landings, there was the bombing of the natural history museum in the town of Caen and, with it, the loss of the Defrance collection, which contained the types for so many of the species named by Lamarck. Even in peacetime, negligence and incompetence have done a lot of damage to natural history collections. In the last thirty years, changes in what university research regards as scientific priorities have been responsible for a number of scandals. To "make room," collections (and even entire libraries) have been purely and simply disposed of by laboratory directors who do not have an interest in, or knowledge of, the natural sciences and lack a sense of history as regards their institutional responsibility. The examples of this are too recent for me to dare mention specific cases in this book. No branch of human activity is free of people who display courage, generosity, and foresight, and others who unfortunately demonstrate only avarice, greed, and stupidity.

The long history of museums such as the Muséum national d'histoire naturelle, in Paris, the Museum of Comparative Zoology at Harvard, or the Academy of Natural Sciences of Philadelphia, combined with a solid tradition of scientific exploration, are reasons why these museums house the types of so many species originating from all over the world. With around 10,000 types of mollusks each, these three institutions as well as a few others, such as the National Museum of Natural History in Washington D.C., form a cohort of centers of reference, although they come a long way behind the Natural History Museum in London (with 27,000 types). The number of types and the diversity of geographical regions from which they come mean that researchers from all over the world ask to consult the types. For those able to travel next door, that is no problem. But how can one deal with a type consultation from a researcher in Argentina, New Zealand, or South Africa? You can't tell them: "Hop on a plane and come spend an hour in Paris, the time it will take to examine the type." Thanks to e-mail and digital imaging, the methods for consultation of types have changed considerably. In one case out of two, a digital image will be enough for a researcher to see what is needed to and find out exactly what the name refers to. Yet there remain numerous cases in which

Pages 94–99.
Do not let yourself be confused by the West Indian "lambi", a conch that is not the same as the strombs of the genus Lambis. *The former is* Strombus gigas *Linnaeus, 1758, whereas the latter are the spider conchs or "pterocera" of the collectors. The scorpion spider stromb,* Lambis scorpius *(Linnaeus, 1758) (above, and on pages 98–99; Philippines, 122 mm [4¾ in.]) is quite common, whereas* Lambis cristinae *Bozzetti, 1999 (pages 94–95 and 96–97 (below); Madagascar, 164 mm [6⅜ in.]) is extremely rare. The validity of the latter species is controversial, and some specialists consider it to be a hybrid. Only new research in the field will make it possible to settle the question, but in all cases the holotype illustrated will remain the name-bearer that defines the application of the name* L. cristinae. *A holotype specimen is unique, conferring a universal scientific value to it. Incidentally, a paragraph in the International Code of Zoological Nomenclature, entitled "Institutional responsibility," recommends that "every institution in which name-bearing types are deposited should make them accessible for study."*

97

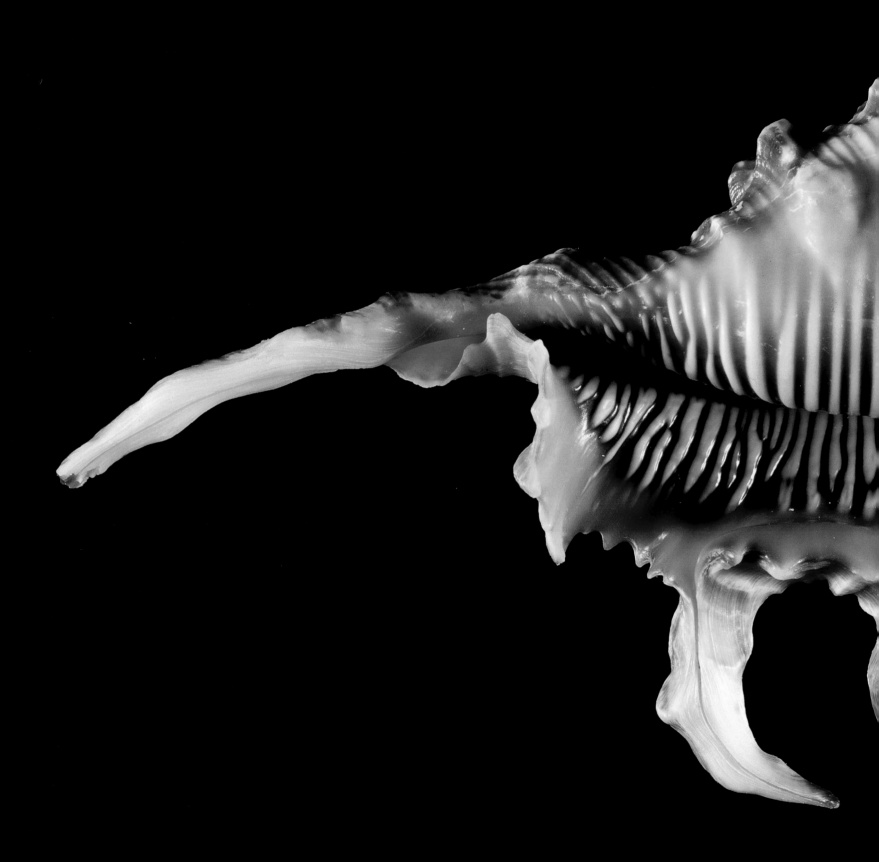

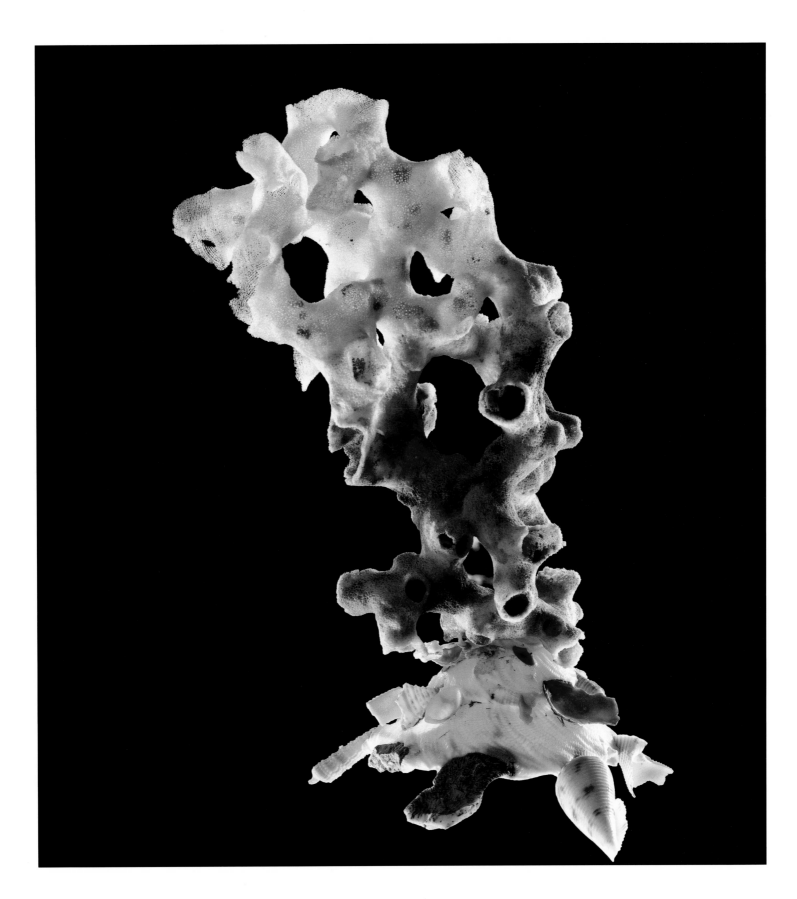

THE ROLE OF NATURAL HISTORY MUSEUMS

an examination of the subject itself is necessary. Museums therefore send out types on loan, and curators have to ensure that the borrower has the legitimate need and skills to manipulate them, and that the loaned specimens do not run a risk of being damaged or lost. The types are carefully wrapped and then sent out by registered mail or, in exceptional cases, through the diplomatic pouch.

At the Paris museum, Virginie Héros is the high priestess who guards the sanctuary of our type bank. No type is entered until she has checked its status with the original description and the Code of Nomenclature; no type is allowed to leave the premises unless it is with her consent, accompanied by a loan form. The type bank is a condensed version of two and a half centuries of exploration by naturalists. It is reminiscent of those momentous times of the voyages of discovery, when Nicolas Baudin discovered and mapped Western Australia, named the Bonaparte Archipelago and Cape Naturaliste, and brought back to France *Trigonia margaritacea* Lamarck, 1804; when Jules Dumont d'Urville commanded the *Astrolabe* on its voyage in 1826–29, during which *Purpura ascensionis* Quoy & Gaimard, 1833 was discovered; when Jean-Baptiste Charcot led the Second French Antarctic Expedition (1908–10), which led to the discovery of *Harpovoluta charcoti* (Lamy, 1910) in the South Shetlands. The type bank also reads like a *Who's Who* of French malacology, containing the types of specialists—Edgar de Boury and his wentletraps, the Marquis de Folin and his *Caecum* species—and of generalists such as Gérard-Paul Deshayes, Hippolyte Crosse, and Félix Jousseaume, who described numerous species across the whole spectrum of molluscan diversity.

In fact, the museum collections continue to be enriched with a hundred different types of mollusks every year. An important share comes from expeditions in the South Pacific. Many new mollusks have consequently been brought from New Caledonia (including *Serratifusus lineatus* Harasewych, 1991; *Conus gondwanensis* Röckel & Moolenbeek, 1995;

Page 100.
This oyster specimen was collected by François Péron during Captain Baudin's historical voyage of discovery to the coasts of New Holland, as Australia was then called. The bizarre warty shell struck both Lamarck when he named it Ostrea tuberculata *in 1804, and Harold Harry when he established the genus* Pustulostrea *for it in 1985.*

Page 101.
In addition to the foreign shells that it collects on itself (see pages 50–51), Xenophora pallidula *(Reeve, 1842) can also serve as a substrate for sponges or corals; certain specimens are covered in improbable scaffolding, which, however, one must imagine being supported by the buoyancy of the seawater.*

Fautrix aquilonia Marshall, 1995; *Dentimargo spongiarum* Boyer, 2001; *Rocroichtys perissus* Sysoev & Bouchet, 2001; *Volutomitra ziczac* Bouchet & Kantor, 2004; *Fusinus laviniae* Snyder & Hadorn, 2006), as well as from Vanuatu (*Scabrotrophon inspiratum* Houart, 2003), Tonga (*Bayerotrochus poppei* Anseeuw, 2003), Indonesia (*Nassaria termesoides* Fraussen, 2006), the Philippines (*Claviscala pellisanserina* Garcia, 2003), and Madagascar (*Calliotropis pulvinaris* Vilvens, 2006). Ever since the work of Michel Adanson (1727-1806), West Africa has been another region in which the Paris museum occupies a place of international significance. The type bank is a showcase for discoveries that continue to be made there, such as *Elachisina pelorcei* Rolan & Gofas, 2003 from Senegal or *Joellina dosiniformis* Cosel, 2006 from Angola. Another source of enrichment for the type bank is the activity of collectors and enthusiasts, mainly Europeans, who choose our museum to deposit new types of species that they are describing. As proof of the intense activity that exists in the field of taxonomy, and with thanks to the generous donors, I would mention the auger shell *Impages escondita* Terryn, 2006 and the cerith *Pseudovertagus elegans* Bozzetti, 2006 (both from Madagascar); the tun shell *Tonna oentoengi* Vos, 2005 (from the Arafura Sea); the cowrie *Cypraeovula kesslerorum* Lorenz, 2006 (from South Africa); the prestigious volute *Lyria bondarevi* Bail & Poppe, 2004 (from Saya de Malha Bank); the tiny marginellid *Cystiscus vitiensis* Wakefield & McCleery, 2006 (from Fiji); the colombellid *Mitrella tosatoi* K. & D. Monsecour, 2006 (from Martinique); the miter *Vexillum alvinobalani* Suduiraut, 1999 and the cone *Conus guidopoppei* Raybaudi, 2005 (both from the Philippines). Of course, many more remain to be discovered in the oceans, and the type bank is not merely a showcase for past research.

Collectors and the Environment

Page 104.
Through the construction of dams, pollution from agriculture, and dredging of riverbeds, the rivers of the United States have changed dramatically since the Frenchman Constantine Rafinesque explored Tennessee and Kentucky, sometimes accompanied by the famous ornithologist John Audubon. Dozens of species of freshwater mussels, including the northern riffleshell, Epioblasma torulosa *(Rafinesque, 1820), have become extinct. The freshwater courses of North America have paid a heavy price for development. West Virginia, 75 mm (3 in.).*

Pages 105–07.
Giant abalone once abounded in the cold waters off the California coast. They were overfished in order to supply restaurants and are now commercially virtually extinct. Haliotis fulgens *Philippi, 1845 is being reared through aquaculture programs. California, 185 mm (7¼ in.).*

Shell collectors may have to defend conflicting views. On the one hand, they tend to cherish and boast about a rare or exceptional species or specimen from their collection because such rarity gives greater value—prestige, of course, but also actual monetary value—to the asset they own. As a first approximation, it could be stated that, like old coins or stamps, a shell would be more valuable the rarer it is. On the other hand, we live in a society that is worried about its impact on the environment. Whalers, wild game hunters, and the collectors of wild orchids do not get good press. Shell collectors do not like to be seen as villains who endanger the survival of the species they are collecting. Collectors' circles are quick to point out that there is no such thing as a rare species, that there are only species whose habitat is unknown and that any species reputed to be rare will one day be found to be common in a habitat that remains to be discovered. They like to cite the example of the cowrie *Cypraea fultoni,* found off the shores of South Africa, and long considered to be very rare, since it was only known through a few specimens found in the stomachs of deep-water fish that was occasionally brought to the surface in trawler's nets. The rarity of the species suddenly became quite relative when Russian fishing boats began trawling off the coasts of Mozambique; in addition to fish and scampi, which they were aiming for, their nets caught hundreds of *Cypraea fultoni.* Is the fate of every "rare" species to be that of *Cypraea fultoni*? That might be believed when you look at the collapse of the value of famous shells in the history of conchology.

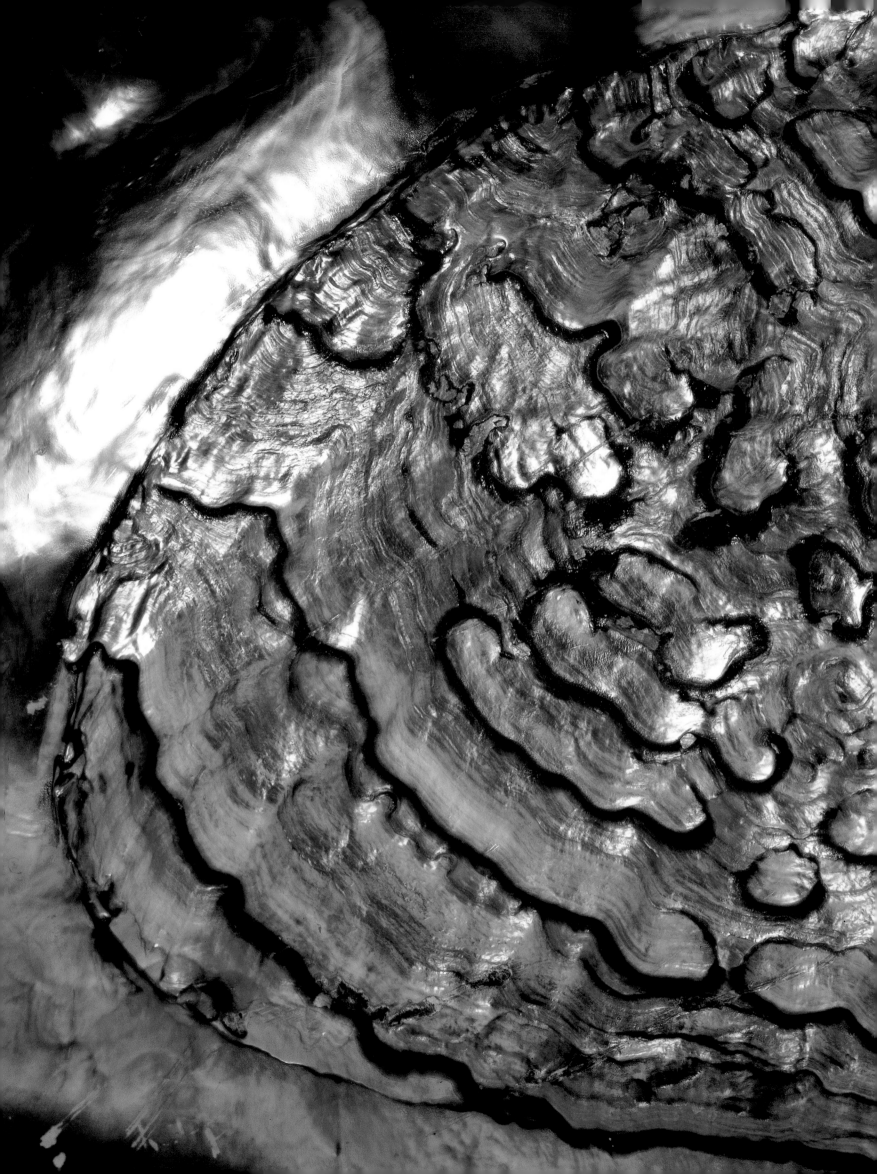

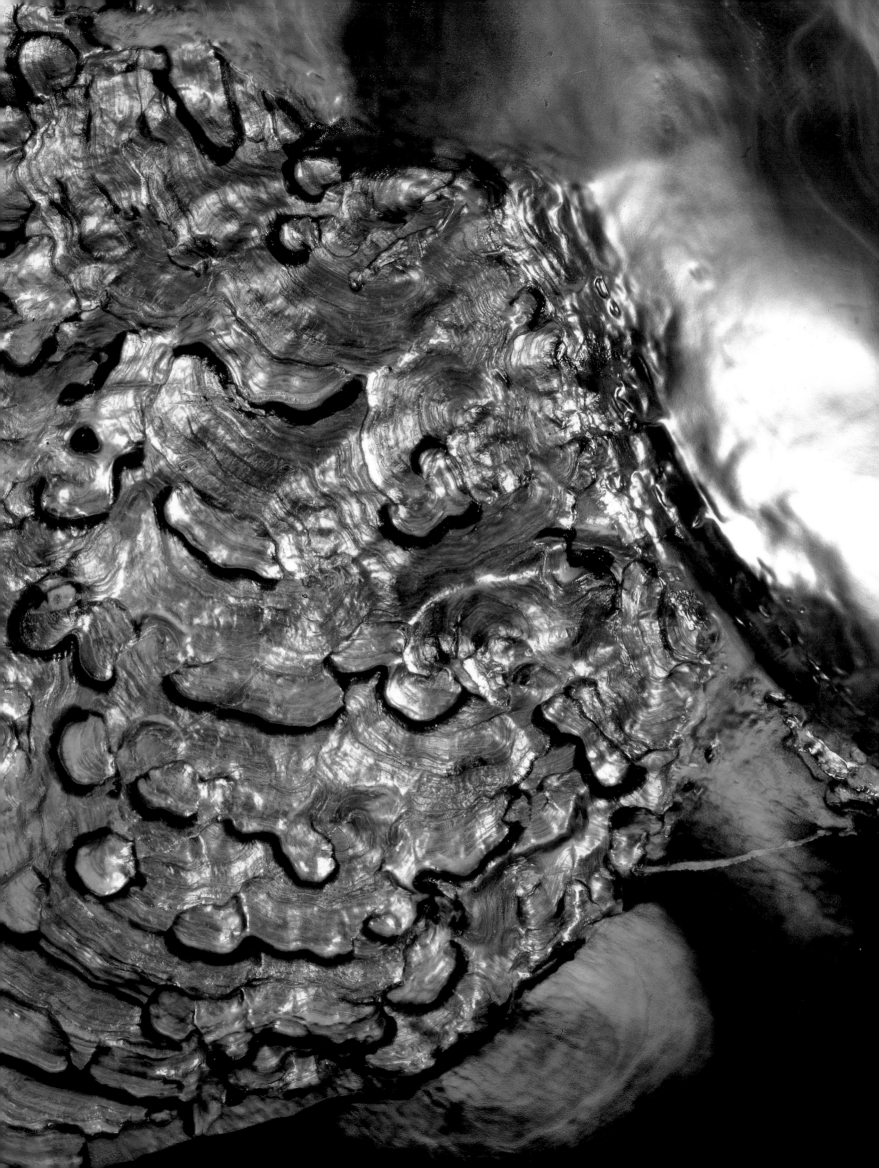

There was a time when you had to be a king, a prince, or a captain of industry to be able to own a *Cypraea aurantium*, the Golden Cowrie, *Conus gloriamaris*, the Glory of the Seas Cone, or *Epitonium scalare*, the Precious Wentletrap (or staircase shell) from the seas off China. Today, these species are within the reach of any collector, even a beginner, as habitats have been discovered in which they are not rare.

Notwithstanding these often quoted examples, the issue of rarity deserves a closer examination. For a dozen years now, I have been leading major expeditions to inventory the mollusk fauna at various points in the tropical Pacific Ocean, off New Caledonia, Vanuatu, and the Philippines. At each site, I have brought together a very large team of scientists and volunteers, and we have deployed a very full array of sampling approaches, including a submarine vacuum cleaner, brushing baskets, and dredges; we collect at low tide and by scuba, during daytime and at night, and so on. Each of these marine biology "workshops" represents an unprecedented sampling effort in the history of the exploration of marine biodiversity. If any research operation could dispel the myth of a "rare" species, it would be this one. And yet the end result has been exactly the opposite. At the Koumac site, on the west coast of New Caledonia, our group sampled 130,000 specimens of mollusks, representing around 3,000 species. In theory, that ought to represent an average of fifty specimens per species, and one can imagine that the abundance of the total catch would form a bell curve, with a small number of rare species counterbalancing a small number of abundant species, on either side of the bell consisting of species that are neither rare nor common. In practice, when Pierre Lozouet analyzed the statistics produced from our observations, he discovered that there is a very small number of abundant species, represented by hundreds, or even thousands, of specimens; there was also a strong contingent of fairly common species, represented by several dozen specimens.

What was unexpected, however, is that despite an unprecedented sampling effort, our work shows that most species are rare or even very rare. Forty-eight percent of the species were represented by five specimens or fewer, and 20 percent were even represented by a single specimen. As Lozouet has explained, with a keen sense of paradox, "rarity is burgeoning." Far from being

COLLECTORS AND ENVIRONMENT

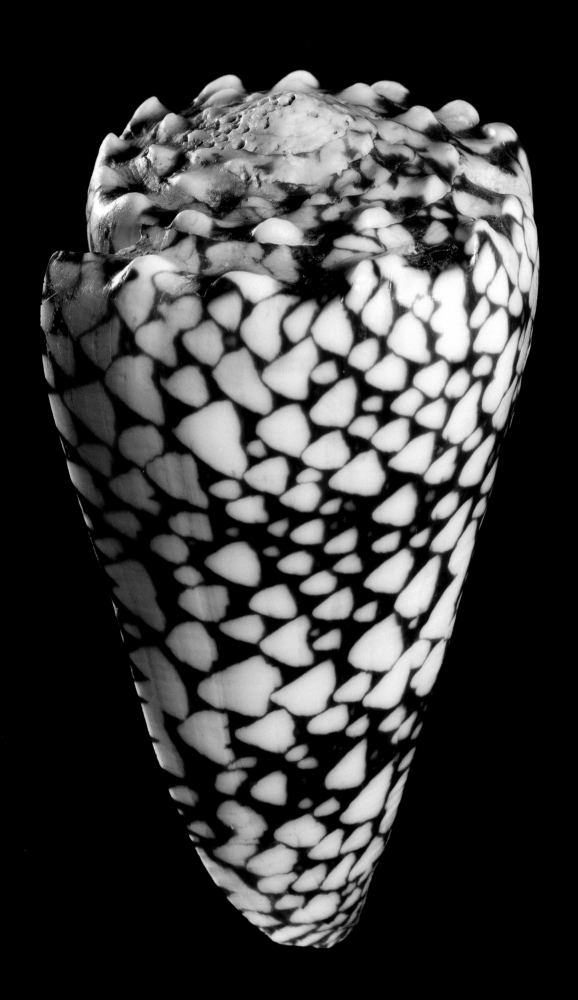

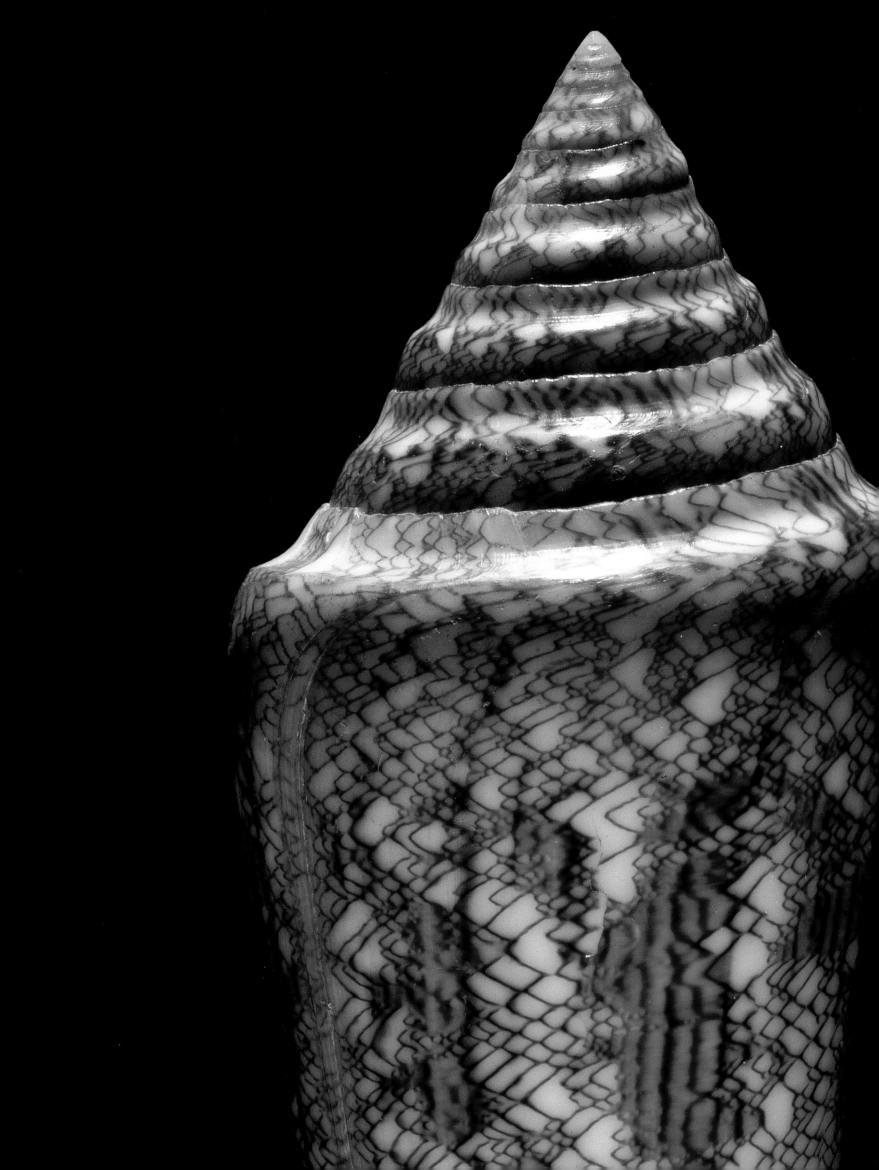

exceptional or anomalous, the results we produced with the Koumac mollusks are similar to those of other researchers working on completely different biological communities. Whether one studies the diversity of insects in tropical rainforests or the diversity of microorganisms in plankton, the same results emerge. On the surface of our planet, most species are rare.

Does this mean that the cries of alarm concerning the disappearance of species are unfounded, or does it mean the opposite, that most species are threatened with extinction? Assuredly, neither is the case, because we are referring to different forms, or different levels, of rarity. If the Caspian Sturgeon, the California condor, or the tiger are currently on the World Conservation Union's Red List of Endangered Species, it is because their numbers have collapsed severely since the late nineteenth century. They diminished under the pressure of hunting, fishing, and change to their habitats. In other words, they *became* rare due to human pressure. In the case of the mollusks of the coral reefs of Koumac, the beetles of the rainforest, or microorganisms in offshore plankton, it is a case of species that are *naturally* rare on our scale of observation. They are objectively rare in the section of reef or jungle that is being studied. However, despite the intensity of the research conducted by our team at Koumac, we managed to comb in total just over a hectare (two-and-a-half acres) of the lagoon and barrier reef. The reason why we scoured only a few square meters with the underwater vacuum device here, or dredged a few dozen square meters of sand there, is that every collecting event is followed by dozens of hours spent at the microscope to pick microshells from the catch. Given that the area studied extended over 30,000 hectares (75,000 acres), a simple calculation would project that even the species represented in our sampling by a single specimen ought to yield some 30,000 individuals in the study area. On the scale of New Caledonia, which is itself only a speckle in the immensity of the Pacific, that would make more than a million individuals for a "very rare" species. It is intuitive to surmise that such "rare" species are not threatened with extinction as long as their environment is not destroyed or damaged.

Are there not species of seashells that are threatened with extinction? This question naturally comes to mind after this disconcerting assertion that states that most species are rare, but that rarity in no way signifies risk of disappearance. The Red List of species threatened with

Pages 112–14.
Cowries and cone shells are favorites of collectors. A beginner's collection will soon include Conus bandanus *Bruguière, 1792 (page 112; Indian and Pacific oceans, 70 mm [3 in.]) and* Conus generalis *Linnaeus, 1767 (page 114; Indian and Pacific oceans, 70 mm [3 in.]). However, for all collectors, owning a specimen of* Conus gloriamaris *Chemnitz, 1777 (page 113; Philippines, 105 mm [4¼ in.]) has long been only a distant dream. Discovered in the mid-eighteenth century, only a dozen specimens of the Glory of the Seas Cone had been found even a century later. Its rarity even led the British conchologist James Cosmo Melvill to assume, in 1884, that the species was "almost as completely extinct as the great penguin or the dodo." Today, several dozen, and even several hundreds, are fished up every year, but the species retains its aura of its past rarity.*

extinction includes only four species of marine mollusks that have become extinct since the nineteenth century, as opposed to around three hundred in land and freshwater mollusks. Yet it will be remembered that there are almost twice the number of species of marine than land and freshwater mollusks, which means that the rate of extinction is two hundred times higher in land and freshwater than in marine species. The proportion is the same in fish. There are roughly the same number of species of fish in the sea as there are in freshwater, but a hundred or so freshwater fish have become extinct, and none in the sea. Some marine conservation advocates have tried to criticize these figures by claiming that they do not reflect reality, because it is much harder to ascertain extinction in the sea than on land, and so extinction in the oceans must be very much underestimated. I won't deny the fact that it is hard to assess extinction in the sea, but critics seem to forget another particularly important point that adds to this difficulty. For an extinction to be included on the Red List, it obviously needs someone who speaks for it, someone who can state: "I know this species, I have looked for it in the right place, using the appropriate means, I have not found it, and I think it is extinct." The whole difficulty of "counting extinction" lies in this series of assertions. If you take birds, there are thousands of experts, both professional and amateur, and every, or almost every, species is being monitored in real time by such organizations as BirdLife International. In the case of invertebrates in general, and mollusks in particular, the number of specialists capable of saying: "I know this species" is in most cases between zero and five. There is a crisis of expertise, and this crisis is particularly acute in the case of land mollusks. Thousands of species of land snails have not been seen for a hundred years, and yet they are not listed as being extinct, because quite simply there is no one around to make the assertion: "I know this species, I looked for it in the right place, using the appropriate means, I have not found it, and I think it is extinct." The three hundred land and freshwater and the four marine species recorded as extinct are without doubt an underestimation of the global situation, but in my view there is no bias in favor of or against the oceans. It is a fact: the extinction of marine species is still an exceptional phenomenon even though the biodiversity crisis has already caused ravages on land and in freshwater. There is no case of a marine species extinction for which shell collectors can be blamed.

Pages 116–17.
The land snails living on oceanic islands have been frontline casualties in the biodiversity crisis, with several hundred species already having become extinct. The fault lies not with collectors, but with a series of historical causes. In the first place, their distribution area had always been miniscule (without a "backup" population to buffer the decline), leaving these species particularly vulnerable to loss of habitat and the introduction of competing or alien species. Saint Helena, despite its iconic isolation (the island still has no airport), is a sad symbol of an ecosystem ravaged by the indifference of eighteenth- and nineteenth-century mariners. Chilonopsis aurisvulpina *(Holten, 1802), endemic on this island, now exists solely in museum collections.
Saint Helena, 45 mm (1¾ in.).*

Are shell collectors thus right to claim that their activity is not a threat to the survival of the species they are collecting? Shell-collecting is like hunting. Setting aside the moral judgments relating to these activities, collecting shells or butterflies and plants for herbariums is only dangerous at the moment when the pressure of the hunt or collection fever becomes greater than the numbers of the target species can stand. Put bison and millions of Native Americans on the plains of North America, and you can maintain an ecological balance for millennia. Take the same bison and replace the Native Americans with a few thousand European hunters armed with rifles, and you bring the bison to the edge of extinction in a few decades. The same is true of shells. The pressure to harvest rare shells is, overall, insignificant in view of the huge distribution area and demographic statistics of the species, and the collection of shells does not, in itself, constitute a threat to their survival. In a few cases, however, seashells have very restricted distributions, which makes them intrinsically vulnerable. This is the case with the cone shells of the Cape Verde Islands. Each island, each bay, has one or more unique species of cones. In total, the archipelago harbors thirty species that live nowhere else in the world. These cone shells are not particularly beautiful in themselves, but their very small geographical habitat makes them "rare" species that are particularly desirable for any cone collector. For the past thirty years, year after year, a succession of collectors and shell dealers has been visiting the Cape Verde Islands. The species of cones there have become rarer and the specimens are smaller than thirty years ago because all are harvested before they have reached full maturity. Certainly, in the case of the cone shells of the Cape Verde Islands, no one other than collectors can be blamed, and it is only as they are "rare" that they are so coveted by collectors.

COLLECTORS AND ENVIRONMENT

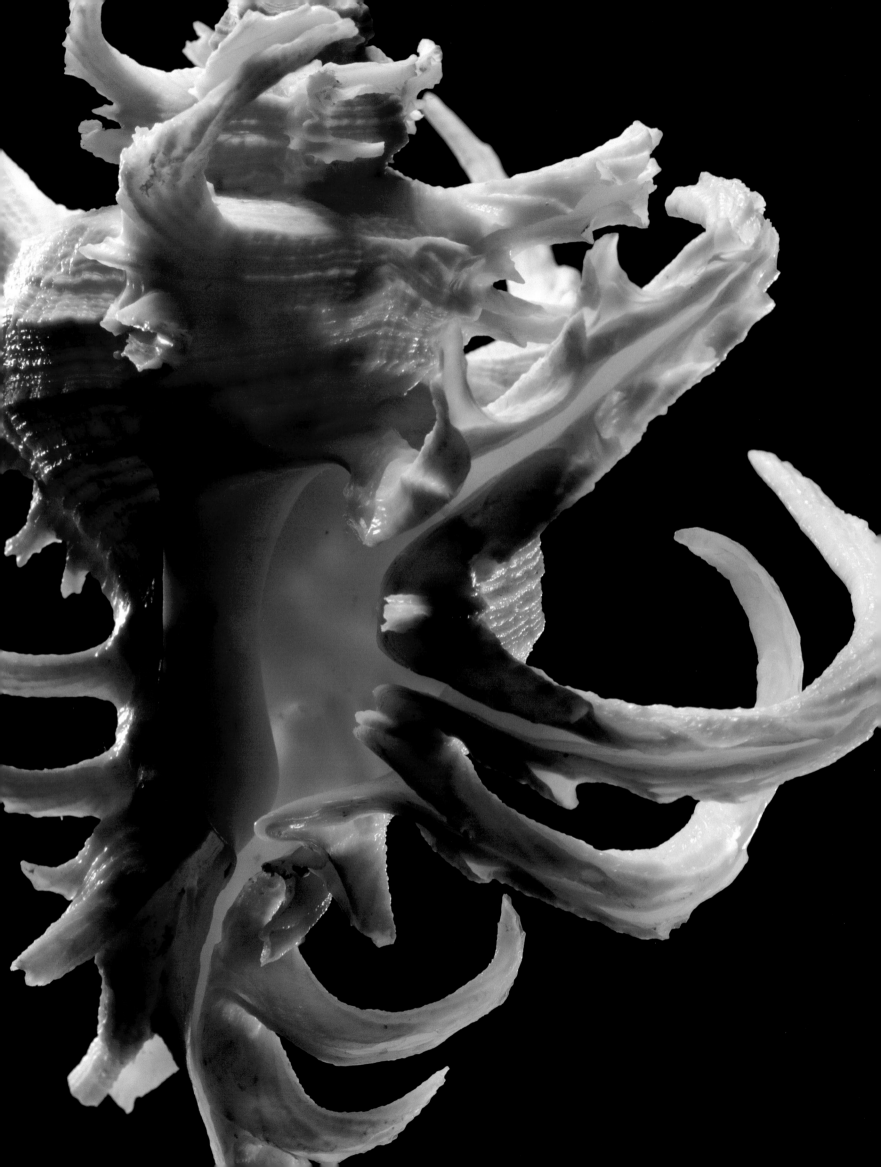

I would have no difficulty in supporting the idea that a moratorium on collecting and trading in cone shells from the Cape Verde Islands is necessary. However, there needs to be not only scientific data, but also sufficient political pressure, for a species to be included on the list maintained by CITES, the Convention on International Trade in Endangered Species of Wild Fauna and Flora. Such a pressure does not exist, unfortunately, because the cone shells of the Cape Verde Islands are not newsworthy enough to capture the attention of the groups that lobby and influence the agenda and decision-making process at the conferences of the countries that are signatories to the convention.

In fact, only two groups of seashells feature in Appendix 2 (species whose trade is regulated but not forbidden) to the CITES. These are the species of giant clams (six species of *Tridacna* and two of *Hippopus*) and the queen conch, *Strombus gigas*, of the West Indies. It should be recognized, however, that it is not the shell trade that threatens these species. The giant clams and the conchs are included on the list because they are gourmet food; their farming is still limited (in the case of the giant clams) or nonexistent (in the case of the queen conch), and it is the wild stocks that have been and continue to be fished almost to extinction. This having been said, the CITES governs international trade and nothing else. The absurdity and hypocrisy of the rules mean that, all over the Pacific, restaurants serve tourists giant clam salads, and lambi (lambi is the local name of the queen conch) stew is one of the gastronomic delights of Guadeloupe and Martinique. Under the CITES, all this is perfectly legal as long as no border is being crossed. On the other hand, no tourist can bring back the odd giant clam shell from Tahiti or Cebu unless it is accompanied by a CITES permit, or the shell will be confiscated and the traveller will have to pay a hefty fine. There is another species that has aroused a lot of anti-collector passion, even though it is not on the CITES list. This is Triton's Trumpet, *Charonia tritonis*, a marine snail that could be ranked as a "top predator," since it easily grows to 30 or 40 centimeters (12–16 inches) and feeds on starfish and sea cucumbers (holothurians). In the 1970s, especially on the Australian Great Barrier Reef, marine biologists observed local population explosions of the crown-of-thorns, or *Acanthaster planci*, a species of starfish that eats coral. Researchers tried to understand the reason for the demographic proliferation in *Acanthaster*, and they accused shell collectors of having caused it by removing too many individuals of their natural predator, *Charonia tritonis*. By banning trade

Pages 119-21.
The spines on this elegant Chicoreus cornucervi *(Röding, 1798) from Australia appear to be light and flexible like a whirling dervish, but in fact they are hard and brittle like those of the Venus comb murex (page 154).*

Pages 123–27.
Despite their apparent lack of similarity, the cone shells (page 123: Conus bengalensis *Okutani, 1968; Thailand, 106 mm [4¼ in.]; pages 124–26:* Conus imperialis *Linnaeus, 1758; Pacific Ocean, 60 mm [2¼ in.]) and the turrids (page 127:* Turris normandavidsoni *Olivera, 2000; Philippines, 70 mm [2¾ in.]) belong to the same group of gastropods, the toxoglossates, typified by their radula, which works like a hypodermic syringe to inject venom into their prey. Pharmaceutical companies are interested in medical applications for these poisons, known as conotoxins. Prialt, originally discovered in the venom of* Conus magus, *was placed on the market in 2006. It is an analgesic as powerful as morphine but without the latter's side effects. The prospects for research are infinite. There are several hundred species of cones and several thousand species of turrids, each of which makes a poison that is a cocktail of dozens of different molecules.*

in the shell, they thought they would be able to restore the ecological balance between the starfish, the coral, and the snail, but the ban did not bring about the expected results. The trade in *Charonia* shells seemed to have been overestimated, while other causes for the starfish outbreak, such as, for example, the eutrophication of lagoon waters from agricultural waste, which in turn boosted the growth and survival rate of starfish larvae. I do not want to conclude by giving the impression that the protection of *Charonia* is ridiculous and that it does no harm to harvest them. In fact, like every top predator, *Charonia* is never an abundant species, probably taking more than ten years to reach adult size, and it is a good thing to leave it alone where it belongs, in its natural habitat.

If it is difficult to make an "ecological judgment" about collecting shells, that is because the collecting of shells is hardly ever the sole cause, or even the main reason, for the rarification of species. Real estate sprawl; ever-larger burgeoning harbor facilities; industrial pollution; dynamite and cyanide fishing; the extraction of gravel, sand, and other construction materials from the seabed; agricultural and domestic effluents; the plowing of the sea bottom by industrial trawlers—all this has an effect on every compartment of the marine ecosystems, including seashells. Does this absolve the collectors from guilt? Perhaps not entirely, but do not let them become the scapegoats for our disquiet when faced with the ecological health of a planet suffering above all from excessive demographic growth, poverty, and unsustainable development. I realize that my relationship with the world of collectors is complex and my judgment is no doubt not entirely impartial. I maintain friendly relations with a number of amateurs who have become much more than collectors and are now recognized experts in one or another family of shells and contribute significantly to the progress of scientific knowledge. (I have counted that in recent years somewhere

COLLECTORS AND ENVIRONMENT

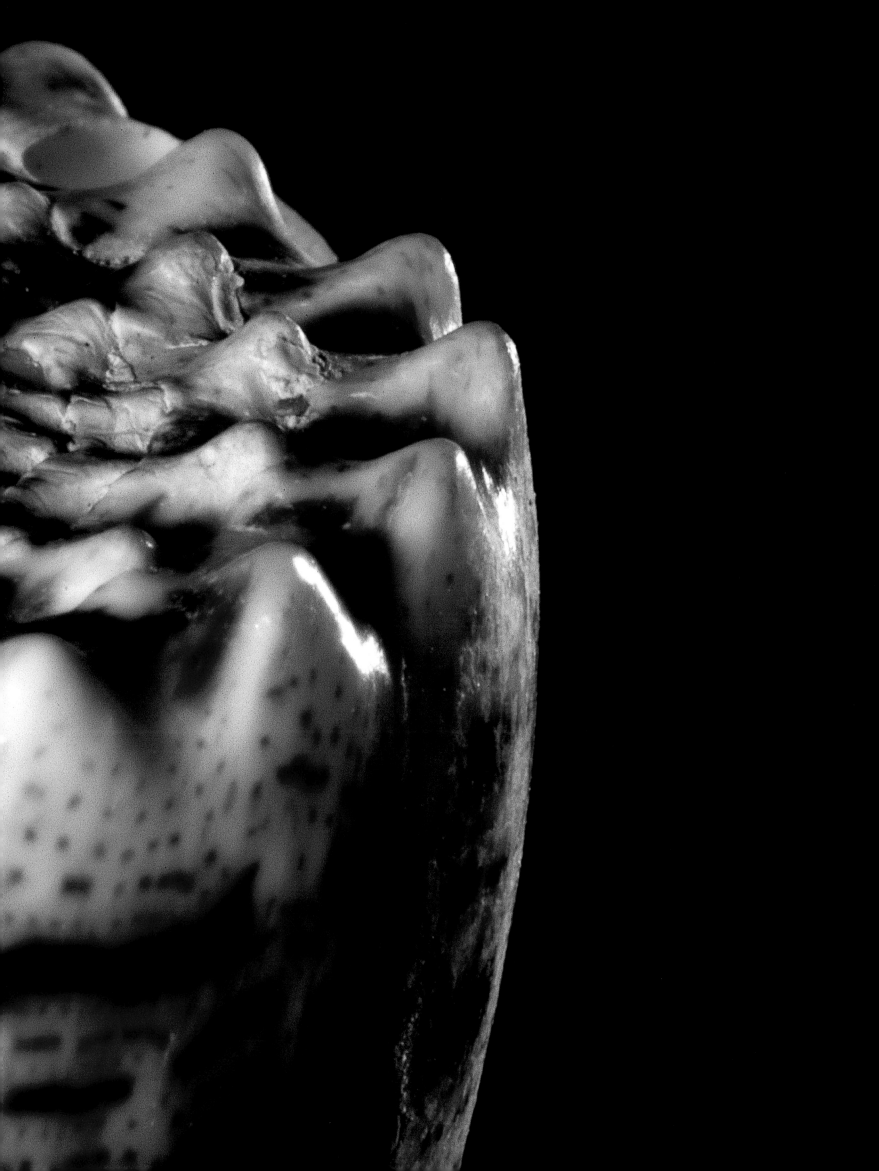

between one-third and half of new marine mollusk species have been described by amateurs.) Amateurs and collectors have even become the main initiators of discoveries in certain regions of the world. In comparison with many other fields of marine zoology, malacology benefits from the luxury of extensive knowledge of the distribution and geographical variability of species. We owe a great deal of this to those generations of passionate enthusiasts and collectors who have been fascinated by the shapes and colors of shells and over the centuries have accumulated—at their own expense and at their own risk—facts and specimens.

The place and impact of amateurs in malacology is frequently compared with those in entomology. The comparison is interesting, but it is limited, because the two disciplines in fact involve the same intellectual processes, the same methods, and the same objectives. A comparison with archaeology would certainly be more stimulating. Even if the market is indisputably responsible for the looting of certain sites and the illegal export of heritage artefacts, it would be excessive to assert that amateurs and collectors have played a negative role in archaeology. What would the major excavation sites be without their volunteers? How could public funding alone support archaeological research, which needs to be supplemented by philanthropy? What would museum collections be like if they could not benefit from donations from inspired and knowledgeable collectors? The role of amateurs in malacology and in entomology is comparable because they also bring skills, labor, and funding, but perhaps what is more important is that through them a wider audience develops empathy and public support for our disciplines.

Pages 128–29.
Like the pustulate cowrie
Jenneria pustulata *(page 136),*
the elongated egg cowrie Volva
volva *(Linnaeus, 1758) belongs*
to the family Ovulidae and feeds
on alcyonarians, or soft corals.
Philippines, 65 mm (2½ in.).

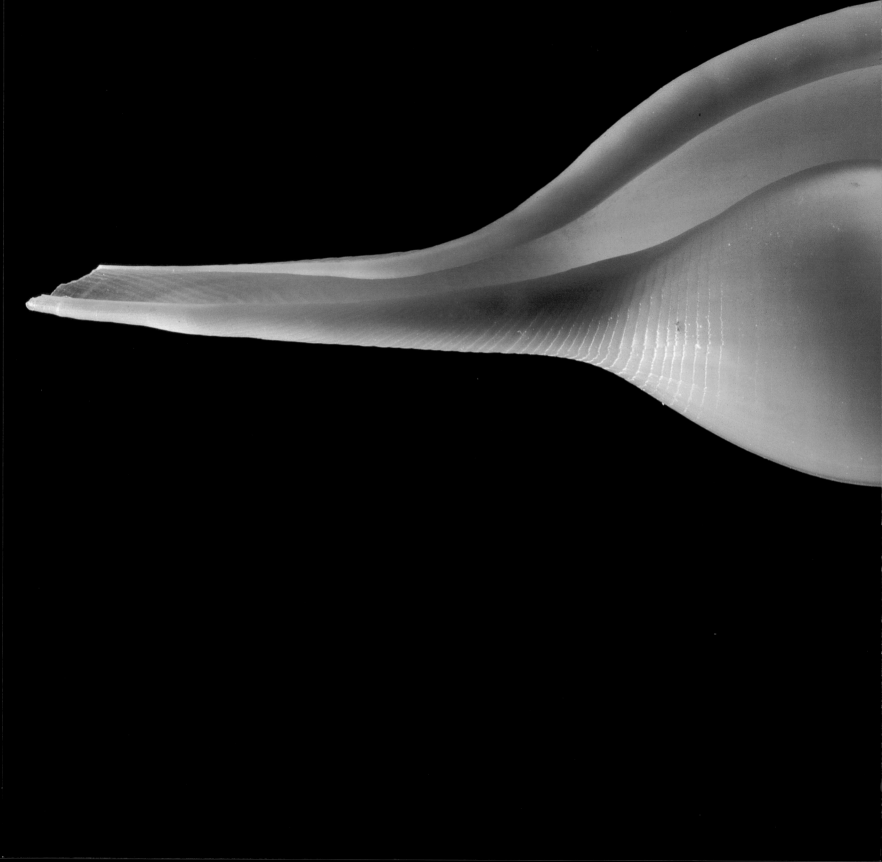

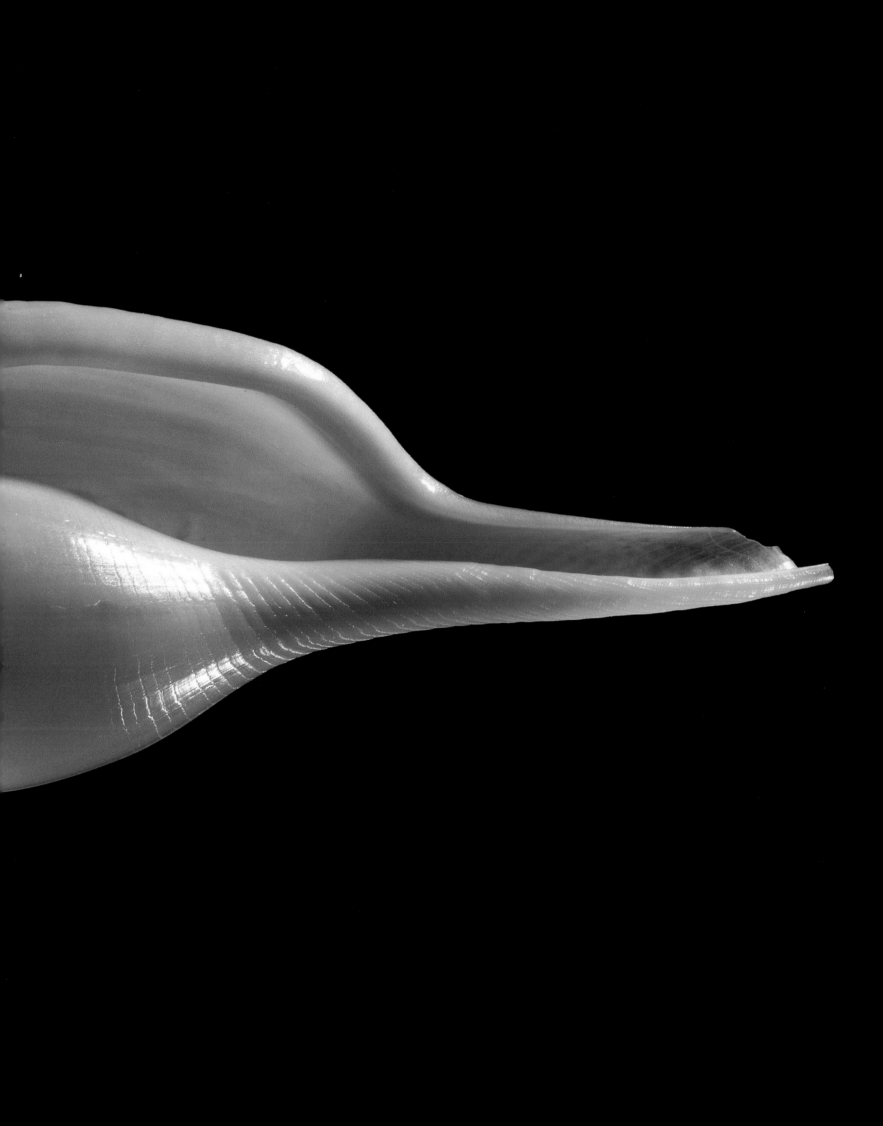

Divergent Views

Pages 130, 133.
When building scientific classifications, species that superficially look like each other may end up being unrelated and vice versa. The Turritella *(page 130:* Turritella duplicata *(Linnaeus, 1758); Philippines, 148 mm [5¾ in.]; page 133:* Turritella terebra *(Linnaeus, 1758); Australia, 73 mm [3 in.]) and the* Vermicularia *(page 150:* Vermicularia spirata *(Philippi, 1836); Caribbean, 120 mm [4½ in.]) are all classified in the family Turritellidae, a family of filter-feeding gastropods. Yet the* Terebridae *(page 151:* Terebra triseriata *Gray, 1834; Philippines, 46 mm [1¾ in.]) are a family of predator gastropods, with a poison gland, like the cone shells (Conidae) and the turrids (Turridae).*

Page 132.
Glossus humanus *(Linnaeus, 1758) is a large bivalve found infrequently on the European continental shelf. The umbos that coil back upon themselves gave it the name of heart cockle in nineteenth-century scientific literature.*
Irish Sea, 70 mm (2¾ in.).

What is the purpose of natural history museum collections? What is the point of storing thousands—thousands? I mean millions—of shells in the drawers of museums? The role of a natural history museum was no doubt obvious in the 19th century and probably up until the 1950s. Back in those days the inventory of fauna and flora grew along with the colonial empires, their natural resources, and their general improvement in well-being. Not infrequently, natural history museums then had departments of Colonial Fisheries, Agricultural Entomology or Economic Botany, or worked closely with laboratories active in those disciplines. During the course of recent decades, the role of natural history museums as existing for the "public good" has found itself being questioned. From one direction, as nature education institutions, museums have found themselves challenged by breathtaking documentaries about animals that appear to have definitively consigned the dusty dioramas and cluttered display cases of the museums' public galleries to their storage basements. From another direction, with regard to research, the extraordinary capacities of molecular biology have caused certain branches of biology, such as the descriptive disciplines of taxonomy, anatomy, and inventorying of flora and fauna to be considered superannuated. Finally, the development of an urban civilization has led a growing number of decision makers, opinion formers, and politicians to abandon the feeling for nature that for so long lay at the root and was the raison d'être of natural history museums.

Traditional natural history museums are now in competition for the attention of the public with science and technology museums and even with factory visits, as well as with natural history exhibits set up in national parks or nature reserves. In the field of biological research, they are outdistanced by such institutions as, in the U. S., the

NOAA (National Oceanic and Atmospheric Administration) or the NIH (National Institutes of Health), whose "usefulness" is obvious to any government administrator or political leader. By contrast, when one contemplates the pitiable state of numerous local natural history museums, it can be seen that the raison d'être of these types of establishments is clearly not evident to the mayor of a city of 500,000 inhabitants. What is the point of maintaining collections of millions of pressed plants, tens of millions of insects, and hundreds of thousands lots of mollusks? This is the very difficulty faced by natural history museums, that of convincing the relevant departments of state and the political leaders responsible for research of their "usefulness." Experience shows that this message is not easy to convey, since those we are trying to convince often lack the culture of curiosity of the naturalist; almost all of those responsible for biology policy in government departments did their training in biomedical research and thus find it much easier to understand the usefulness of research on the molecular receptors of the nervous system.

The collections of natural history museums have a threefold purpose. They are there for scientific, heritage, and educational reasons. These last two, which are shared with art museums, represent the functions that are the most intuitively understood and appreciated by the general public. We have all, at least occasionally, visited a gallery, a monument, or a historical site. The preservation of Albert Einstein's manuscripts, of Charles Lindbergh's *Spirit of St. Louis*, or of the Rosetta Stone is part of this heritage function. Of course, we do not *need* these items in order to be able appreciate the work of the Nobel Prize laureate, retracing the history of aviation, or deciphering hieroglyphics. The manuscripts of Einstein can be consulted online in the form of digital images, faithful reproductions of the machine flown by Lindbergh can be seen in aeronautical museums all over the world, and any visitor to the British Museum can buy a copy of the Rosetta Stone in the museum store. (In fact, it was from a copy—rather than from the original—that Jean-François Champollion made the discoveries that opened the door to our understanding of Ancient Egypt.) So what is the point of preserving the originals? Isn't there something rather incongruous in even asking the question? Don't we, all of us, keep letters, photographs, a trinket, or an item of furniture that is precious to us, to which we attribute an

Isn't the angelwing clam a wonderfully appropriate name? Unfortunately, its scientific name is rather unimaginative and does not match it. The name Cyrtopleura costata *(Linnaeus, 1758) refers to the curvature of its ribs. This large bivalve of the North American Atlantic coast lives buried in sandy mud to a great depth—up to nearly a meter (40 in.) beneath the surface. Once dug out, it is incapable of burying itself again. Size: 167 mm (6½ in.).*

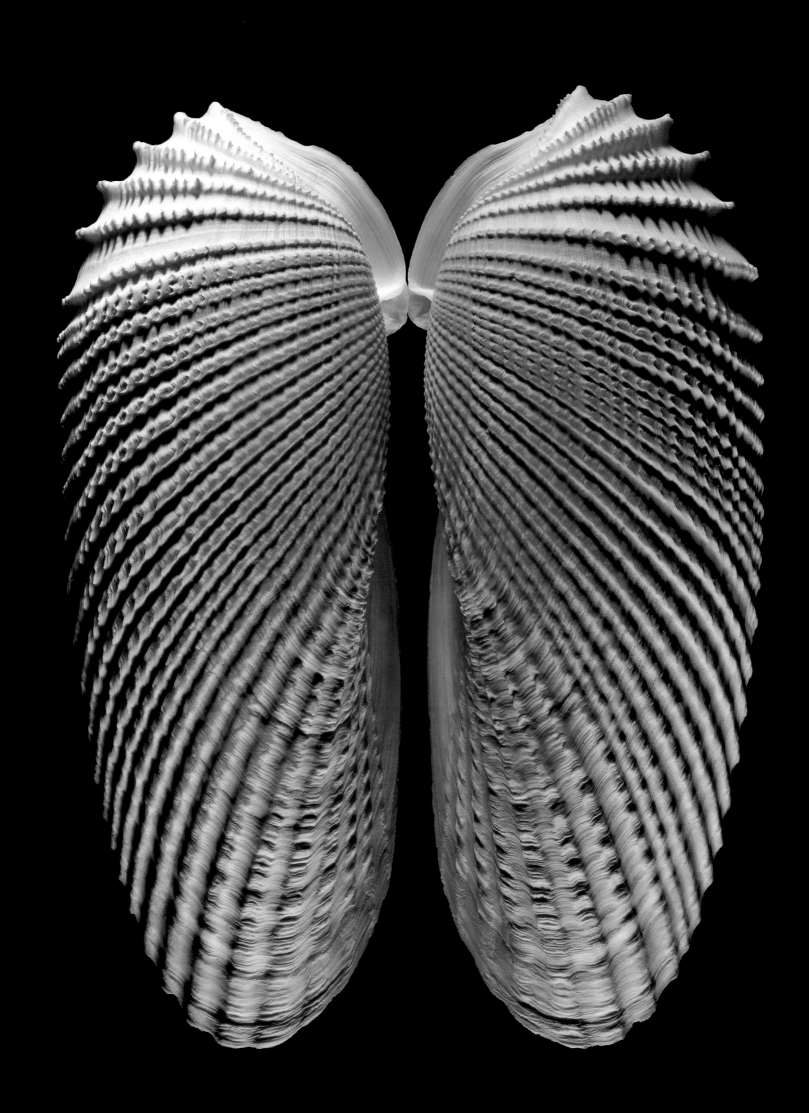

importance that has little to do with its intrinsic commercial value, but whose roots are to be found in our family history or in our own life experiences? These are objects from which we would not be parted "for anything in the world." Collectively, this is the same sentiment that causes us to preserve Thomas Jefferson's home in Monticello, George Washington's false teeth, or the flag that flew at Fort McHenry. When extended to natural history, it is this heritage function that justifies the Paris museum in preserving the collection of shells gathered by Michel Adanson off the coast of Gorée, Senegal, in the mid-eighteenth century, which he represented as engravings in his *Histoire naturelle du Sénégal* [Natural History of Senegal] published in 1757. Nor is there any need to be a malacologist to be aware of the historical value of the shells collected by Marie Jules-César Savigny when, as a member of the Commission des savants, he was part of Napoleon Bonaparte's campaign to Egypt. Nor is it important that most of Savigny's samples do not contain an indication of their geographical origin—are they from the Red Sea or the Mediterranean?—or their ecology—sand or coral reef? Nor is it important that most of these samples are battered and worn shells that even a beginner would reject for his collection. What makes these specimens interesting is obviously neither their aesthetic value nor the quality of the ecological information associated with them.

The major natural history museums are both showcases and research establishments. Like the stuffed beasts on display, the cases of butterflies and moths and the dinosaur skeletons, shells are indisputably part of what the public expects to see during a visit to a natural history museum. But natural history museums are also the place par excellence for taxonomical research. The collections on which the two functions are based—educating the public and the research infrastructure—are in fact of a fundamentally different nature. The main quality required from a collection destined for the public is its educational value. "Educational value" is to be understood as encompassing the delivery of a message or the demonstration of facts, as well as the purely aesthetic quality of an object.

The criteria for judging the aesthetic quality of a shell would appear to be easy to appreciate. To be convinced that this is not necessarily the case, one needs to understand to what extent the growth of the

Pages 136–37.
You think you could recognize a cowrie, don't you? Lightfoot also made that mistake when he described this species as Cypraea pustulata. *Contrary to appearances,* Jenneria pustulata *(Lightfoot, 1786) does not belong to the family Cypraeidae at all, but to the Ovulidae, also known as the false cowries. The two families are actually not closely related and have very different feeding habits. The Cypraeidae graze on algae and sponges, whereas the Ovulidae are carnivorous predators that live on soft corals and sea fans. Eastern Pacific, 21 mm (⅞ in.).*

▷
Nucella lapillus *and* Chimaeria incomparabilis *(pages 140–41) are prime examples of the difference in the way scientists and collectors regard shells. For scientists, the beauty or rarity of a shell is irrelevant. The great advantage of the small dog whelk* Nucella lapillus *(Linnaeus, 1758) is precisely because it is a common species in the tidal zones on both the European and the American shores of the North Atlantic. For this reason, any variation in the number of chromosomes, shell color and shape, number of eggs laid, and so on, are easy to study. As a result, this gastropod has become one of the most intensively studied by marine biologists as they seek to understand the relationship between such variation and the features of its environment.*

specimen seashell market has revolutionized these criteria during the last decades of the twentieth century. At a time when travel was rare, and before scuba diving had been invented, a Venus Comb Murex with a few broken spines or a cone shell whose lip was slightly chipped was acceptable. Today, no serious collector would tolerate such flaws—to be beautiful it must be perfect. Special attention is paid to the size, freshness of the coloration, originality of the color pattern, and perfection of the shell. Each item is carefully cleaned and sometimes coated with paraffin wax to enhance its glaze. From this point of view, the collections in the major museums often seem pale alongside the brilliance of private collections. The specimens exhibited are also chosen on the basis of the message they are supposed to convey. If I want to illustrate the range of feeding habits of gastropods, I will choose an herbivore, a parasite, a predator, a filter feeder, and so on. I may then display two or three examples from each category, but I will certainly not try to show all of the herbivorous species, all of the parasitical species, and so on. In such a collection, comprehensiveness does not matter, and information, whether geographical or ecological, is associated generically with the species exhibited rather than with the exact specimen on display.

This is the very opposite of the criteria that determine the scientific value of a shell. In a scientific collection, the accuracy and quality of the information about the site and the conditions under which a particular specimen was collected are essential, and the label is an integral part of the sample. This is because specimens from museum collections constitute the basis of research in the various areas of systematics and in comparative biology in general (floristics and faunistics, anatomy, functional morphology, biogeography, and evolution). This material also contains remarkable environmental indicators used by a wider scientific community. For example, the carbonate parts of the skeletons and the organic matrix that binds together the shell crystals provide an instant picture of their environment at the moment they were secreted. By analyzing the isotopic ratios of oxygen atoms contained in the composition of the calcium carbonate ($CaCO_3$), the shells of the mollusks make it possible, for example, to measure the temperature of an ocean basin a hundred or a thousand years ago, and thus to retrace the ocean currents and the paleoclimate. Another example of collections as environmental markers is provided by the use of museum specimens to document the impact of pollution. In the 1970s,

Pages 140–41.
It could be claimed that Chimaeria incomparabilis *Briano, 1993 is the most famous shell of the twentieth century. This species is known from only six specimens: three were collected by Soviet ships in the Gulf of Aden in the 1980s and three were collected by commercial shrimp boats operating off the coast of Somalia. One of these specimens came into the hands of the Italian collector and dealer Bruno Briano, who described it and chose to deposit the holotype in the collections of the Paris museum. Due to the political instability in that part of the world, the supply has dried up, and* Chimaeria incomparabilis *remains one of the most coveted shells of our time.*
Size: 80 mm (3¼ in.).

Page 143.
The slipper limpet, Crepidula fornicata *(Linnaeus, 1758), is native on the Atlantic coasts of the U.S., but reached England accidentally with oysters imported from Virginia. From there, it spread to the North Sea and the Bay of Biscay. In the last thirty years, due to the eutropication of coastal waters through agriculture fertilizers, the numbers of the slipper limpet have exploded; it is now a nuisance to the commercial scallop beds. While it is scorned by fishermen, it is valued by scientists studying the endocrine mechanisms that determine sex. That is because this limpet is a protandrous hermaphrodite, i.e., it begins its life as a male and fertilizes females who are lower down in the chain of individuals fixed to the substrate; it then changes sex into a female and is fertilized by newly settled males. Linnaeus was unaware of the biology of this species, and the epithet he gave it,* fornicata, *simply means "vaulted," in reference to the shape of the shell.*
Size: 40 mm (1½ in.).

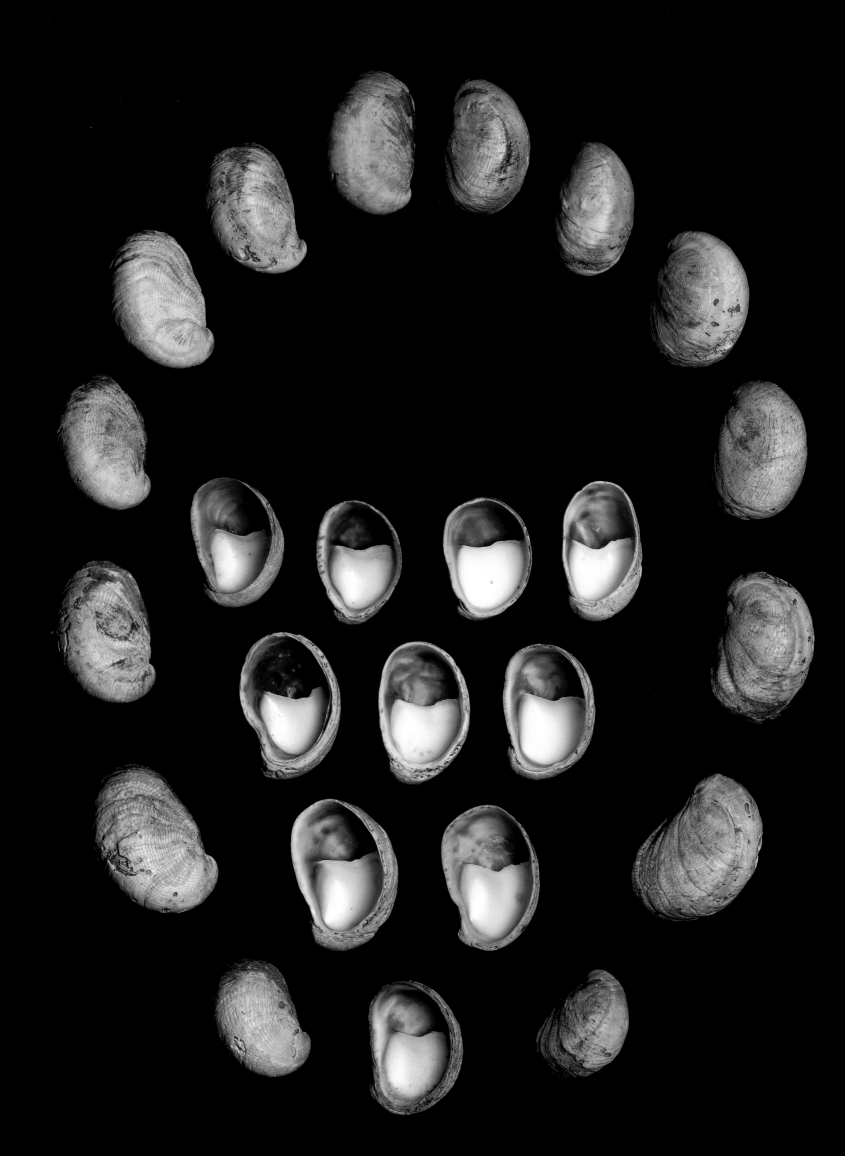

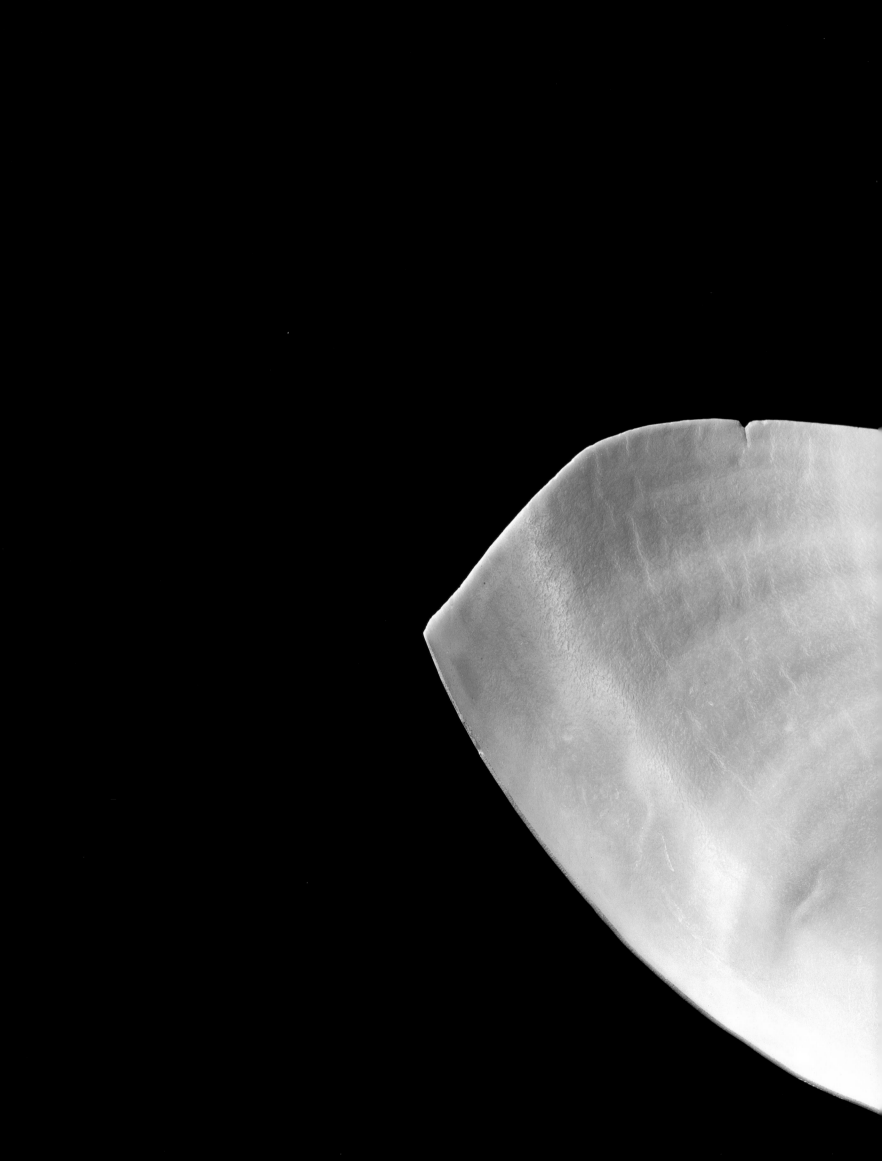

Pages 144–47.

Reference is always made to "the" nautilus, but there are in fact at least three species of nautilus in the world (this one is the Emperor nautilus, Nautilus pompilius *Linnaeus, 1758), plus a few bizarre forms that may be variations of one of these three or species in their own right. With its succession of mother-of-pearl-lined chambers and strange method of locomotion, the nautilus has fascinated artists as well as mathematicians and engineers since the Renaissance. Much has been written about the properties of the nautilus's spiral, of which two successive chambers are reputed to have dimensions in the ratio of 1.618: the famous golden number. This is unfortunately a myth. In fact, the ratio is closer to 1:3. This does nothing to detract from the beauty of the shell. Philippines, 170 mm (6½ in.).*

various gastropods started to display endocrinological disorders that were responsible for pseudohermaphroditism (females began growing male genitalia), also called "imposex"; research established a link between these aberrations and the intensive use of antifouling paints containing tributyltin (TBT), to the point where paint containing this substance is now banned in most developed countries. Yet Mediterranean specimens of *Hexaplex trunculus*, the Banded Dye-Murex, preserved in alcohol in museum collections since the mid-nineteenth century, show that some specimens were already affected by imposex even before the invention of antifouling paints. Research is currently underway to interpret this very recent and unexpected observation.

In a scientific collection, a particular species is not chosen on the basis of its size, coloring, or whether it belongs to a particular family. The species that interest scientists may be ugly, and those that interest collectors may be of no interest to them whatsoever. Out of curiosity, I looked up in the *Zoological Record*, the largest online bibliographic database in the field of zoology, a few of the key species of interest to scientific research and a few of the species that collectors dream about. The divergence of interests is striking. In the first category is *Mytilus edulis* (the blue mussel), which produces 4,438 references, *Nucella lapillus* (the dog whelk), which produces 358, *Littorina saxatilis* (a periwinkle), which offers 342, and *Buccinum undatum* (whelk) 185; whereas in the second category, there are only 6 references to *Cypraea leucodon*, 14 to *Conus gloriamaris*, and to *Chimaeria incomparabilis* . . . just one.

In an amateur shell collection, the species are in principle already all known, and in general, a collector seeks to obtain one or several specimens that are representative of each species of a particular family. The cowries are by far the most frequently collected family, followed by the cone shells, the miters, the volutes, strombs, and a few others. In total, the families collected do not represent more than 3,000 or 4,000 species of shells, i.e., barely 5 percent of the diversity of Mollusca. The purpose of a scientific collection, on the other hand, is to assist the taxonomist in forming hypotheses as to the limits between species and to describe *all* of the biodiversity, without preconceived opinions. This means that, ideally, museums ought to contain samples of populations collected over the whole of the distribution area of every

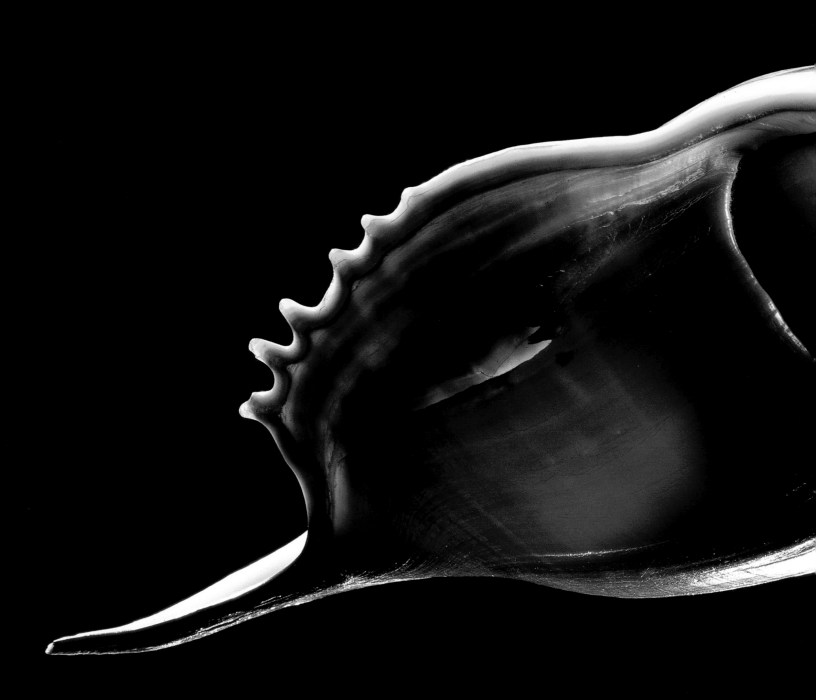

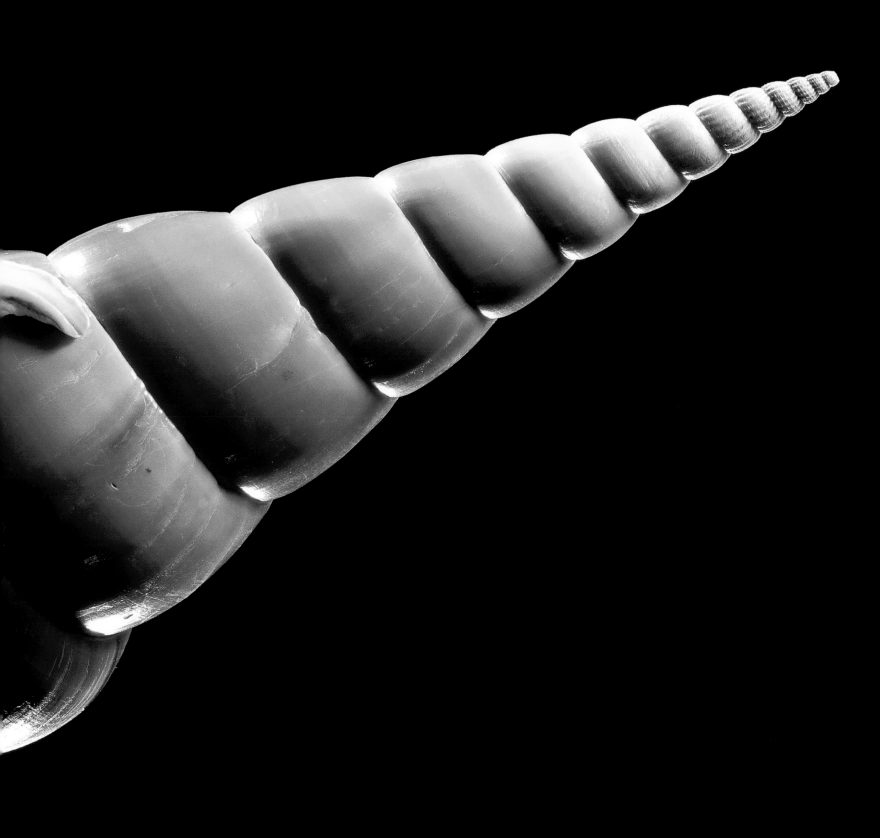

species in every family, without making any preselections other than those dictated by respect for the environment. In such a collection, it matters little whether a particular murex has a few broken spines, or the lip of a cone shell is slightly chipped, because these are not the essential characteristics needed to discriminate between species. Conversely, and unlike a collector, a scientist will assign considerable value to the apex of the shell because the first millimeter of the shell secreted by the larva contains a great deal of information that can be connected to the larval ecology and genetic structuring of the species. In a scientific collection, the shells are generally never cleaned and, in any case, never coated in paraffin wax; the immature specimens are of just as much interest as the adults. Well-documented samples of specimens showing variability within a single population of known origin are of much greater importance than accumulations of single specimens originating from disparate sources.

However, the basic difference between the malacological collections of a museum and the conchological collections of aficionados is in the animal itself. It should not be forgotten that the shell is merely the external envelope secreted by the mantle of a mollusk. All of the classification of the Mollusca is based on the anatomical features of the animal and the molecular characters of its tissues. In a few cases, the early shell-based classifications formulated by the founding fathers of malacology have been corroborated by characters taken from the animal, but it must be realized that in most cases, the shell is not the right instrument for classifying mollusks at the levels of families or orders. As the cost of molecular sequencing has collapsed over the years, the value of the shell of a mollusk as a classification and identification tool is now being challenged also at the level of species. The purpose of a major international program, entitled Consortium for the Barcoding of Life (CBOL), is to associate each living organism with the sequence of the gene coding for the cytochrome oxidase I, which is present

Pages 148–49.
In 1798, Peter Friedrich Röding bestowed the name Tibia insulaechorab *on this shell in a booklet entitled* Museum Boltenianum. *Because of the great rarity of his work in libraries, Röding remained ignored until the early twentieth century. The French, in particular, delayed for as long as possible the moment when the validity of the names he had established had to be admitted. That is because Röding's work predated by several years that of the Frenchman Jean-Baptiste Lamarck. To accept Röding's names would have meant the quasi-sacrilegious abandonment of some of the names suggested by their fellow countryman.*
Gulf of Aden, 190 mm (7½ in.).

Left.
See caption on page 131, top.
Terebra triseriata *Gray, 1834*
Philippines, 46 mm (1¾ in.).

Page 150.
See caption on page 131, top.
Vermicularia spirata
(Philippi, 1836)
Caribbean, 120 mm (4½ in.).

Pages 152–53.
The Distorsio *are remarkable for the extensive development of a parietal shield around the aperture, and their periodic growth. These phenomena combine to give the shells their extraordinary, even grotesque, appearance, particularly in the case of* Distorsio anus *Röding, 1798.*
New Caledonia, 63 mm (2½ in.).

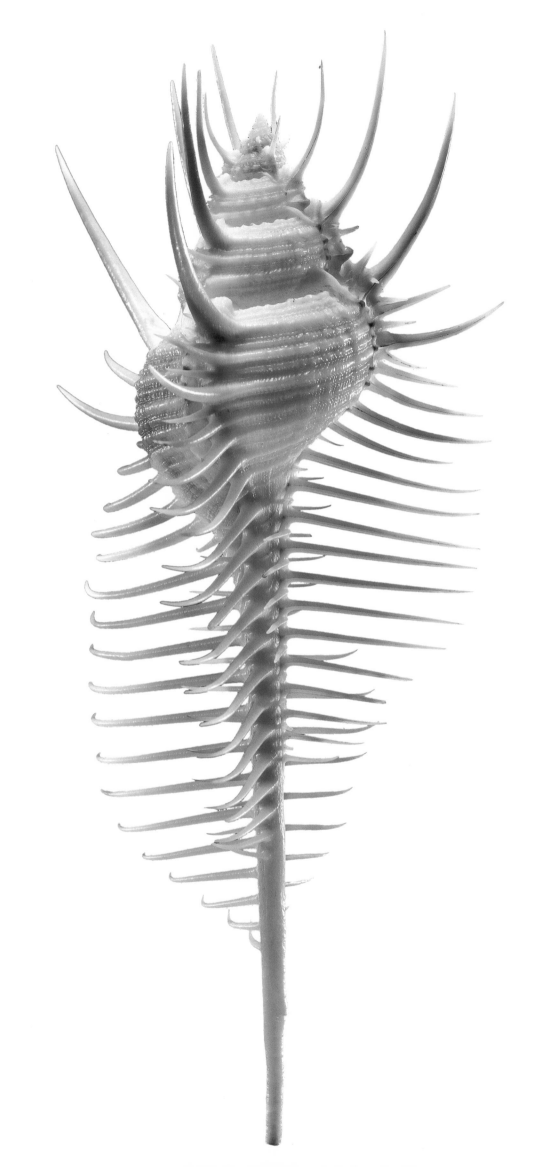

Pages 154–55.
The spines of Murex pecten
Lightfoot, 1786 *inspired con-*
chologists to give it the common
name of Venus comb. Perfect
specimens are taken in the Philip-
pines by tangle nets deployed on
muddy sand.
Size: 137 mm (5¼ in.).

in every species with a species-specific pattern. For malacological collections, this program represents a complete revolution in the way in which we currently constitute collections that will be used for tomorrow's research. The aim from now on is to associate each lot of specimens, or at least each species, with a tissue sample that will be stored in ethanol, from which DNA can be extracted. We are only at the very beginning of this revolution, and we probably do not yet fully appreciate the consequences that it is bound to have on the nature and organization of future collections created for molluscan research.

There was a time when the difference between a research collection and an exhibited collection was tenuous; at that time, the great national natural history museums tried to have "something of everything," for a host of reasons, whether good (slowness of communications between researchers) or bad (competition between museums, each of them trying to become "the biggest"). It is obvious today that when collections are viewed as a research tool, no museum can claim to be the sole repository of samples from populations taken from the entire area of distribution of every species of every family, and to be able to do so for all the phyla of biodiversity. Just as taxonomists have specialties that favor complementarity rather than competition, so the major natural history museums today work together by networking. Admittedly, each museum has its own fields of excellence, in which it fuels research data to scientists throughout the world. Yet Paris, London, and Washington are the three great "generalist" museums. This does not mean that they are "good at everything" and that their researchers can work in splendid isolation; rather it means that the three institutions have something to provide to everyone, regardless of the biogeographical regions and phyla studied. That is obviously something to be proud of, but it is also a pride that comes with strings attached.

Pages 156–57.
Why does the pagoda shell,
Columbarium pagoda *(Lesson,*
1831*), have such a long siphon*
canal? Scientists still know
nothing about the biology of this
member of the Turbinellidae and
the question remains unanswered.
South China Sea, 64 mm
(2½ in.).

So—unexpectedly you might think—*Shells*, and the study of shells, covers almost every field—sociology, history of science, politics, and even international affairs. In this respect, malacology and taxonomy are no different from other branches of knowledge. Having said that, however, I want to point out that the taking of inventories in relation to biodiversity is at a crossroads like no other science. I belong to the first generation of researchers that is aware that there probably remain another 100,000 or 150,000 species of mollusks to be discovered, described, and named, and that half of them will have disappeared from the surface of the planet before the middle or the end of this century. I am constantly torn between the desire to shut myself away selfishly in pursuit of this elusive horizon, the desire to share my exultation and my message concerning the challenges of the biodiversity crisis, and the need to convince the world about the importance of museum collections as a key element in our arms race to combat environmental ignorance.

Pages 159–61.
Throughout the world, rocky shores beaten by the waves are the habitat of limpets, hooded gastropods that cling tenaciously to the rocks and graze on algae, but each region has its specialties. Clypidina notata *(Linnaeus, 1758), also known as the black-ribbed false limpet, lives in the northern Indian Ocean (page 159: Sri Lanka, 11–20 mm [¹⁄₁₆–¾ in.]). South Africa is the land of the* Patella, *such as this eye limpet,* Patella oculus *Born, 1778 (page 160: South Africa, 60 mm [2½ in.]), while the American Pacific Coast, from California to Chile, is the land of the Lottiidae (page 161:* Scurria parasitica *[d'Orbigny, 1846]; Chile, 17 mm [⅝ in.]).*

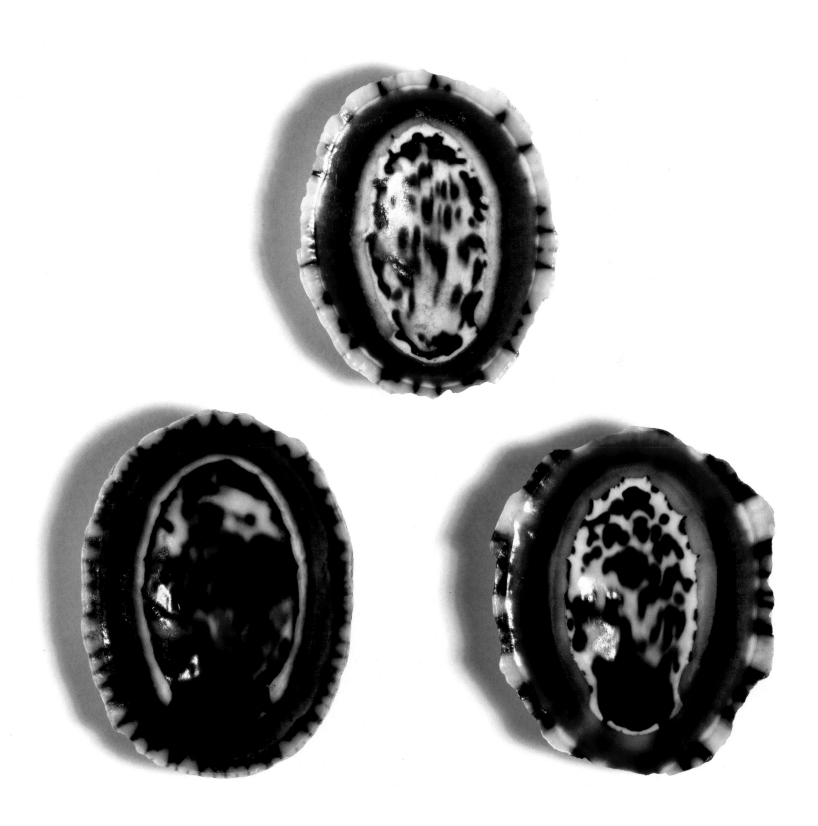

PHOTOGRAPHIC CREDITS AND PHOTOGRAPHER'S ACKNOWLEDGMENTS

The photographs for this book were produced using silver emulsion and a Sinar darkroom, Broncolor flash, and Fujichrome Velvia film (4 × 5 inch format). All the colors are natural, no filters were used.

I should like to offer my warmest thanks to:

Bertrand-Pierre Galey, Director-General of the Muséum national d'histoire naturelle; Philippe Pénicaut, Director of Communication; and Anne Roussel-Versini, editor.

Philippe Bouchet, and his whole team, including Virginie Héros, Joëlle Rameau, Bernard Métivier, Benoît Fontaine and Philippe Maestrati, for their patience, assistance, and advice.

The Dupon photographic laboratory in Paris, its director M. Jean-François Camp, for his support and technical assistance and that of his whole team, including Bénédicte Poupard for her efficient coordination, as well as Éric Martin and James Rousseau for the quality of the development of my photographs.

Fujifilm and the Professional Photography Section, including Bruno Baudry and Franck Portelance, for the encouragement and valuable technical support they provided me in my photographic work.

Janine Seymand, for her patience and the hospitality she showed me when I was taking shots in the studio.

Jean-Marc Dabadie, Director of Éditions de l'Imprimerie nationale—Actes Sud for his support in the project and his determination to see it through, and Annick Harnet-Salm, Publishing Director, for the efficiency of her coordination.

Finally, I must thank Pierre Finot, graphic artist and designer, for the way he listened and the creativity of his layouts.

I have dedicated this book to my children, Iskander and Inès.

—Gilles Mermet

Philippe Bouchet wrote the French version of this book in Washington, DC, in March 2007, and he thanks Ellen Strong, curator of mollusks at the Smithsonian Institution for hospitality, inspiration, and stimulation. He thanks Richard Petit, of North Myrtle Beach, South Carolina, for his advice for the English language edition.

Page 163.
See page 28.
Turris babylonia
Indonesia, 80 mm (3¼ in.).

Pages 164–65.
The winkle Littorina saxatilis *(Olivi, 1792), which is so common along the European coasts of the North Atlantic, is found in only two places in the Mediterranean: the upper Adriatic and the Gulf of Gabès, in Tunisia. That is because these are the only two locations in the Mediterranean that have a significant tidal range. Curiously, Giuseppe Olivi gave this winkle its current scientific name based on specimens from one of these "atypical" localities, the lagoon of Venice, where it had almost certainly been brought by man.*

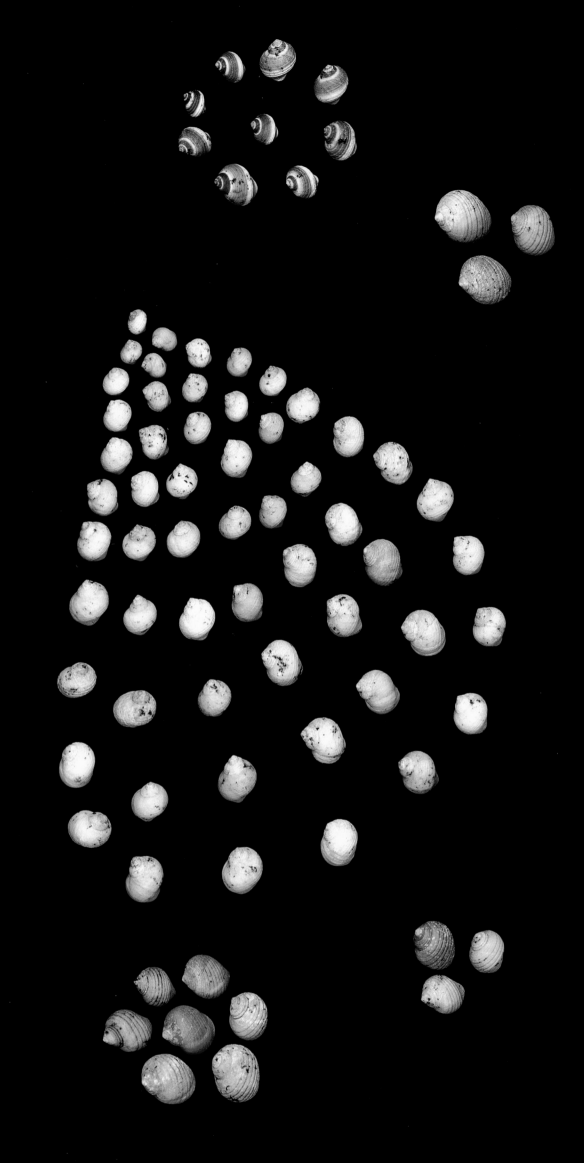

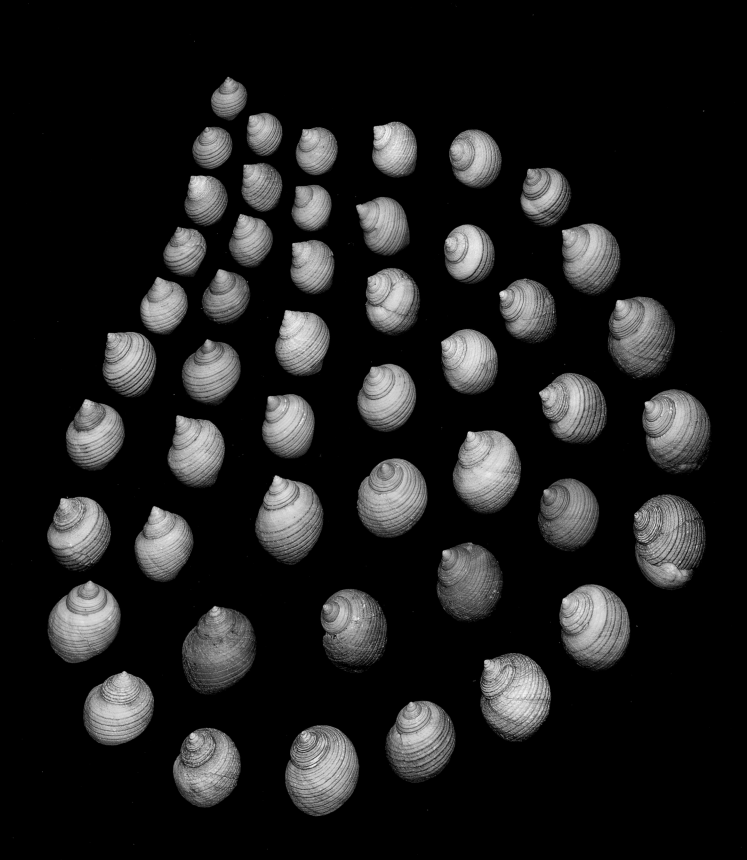

AXIAL: Designating the elements of the sculpture of a shell that extend from the tip toward the base, that is, vertically, when the shell is held with its tip pointing upward and aperture facing the observer. The opposite of *axial* is *spiral*.

BYSSUS: A secretion made by some species of bivalves to attach themselves to rocks, usually (as in the blue mussel) consisting of a bundle of hairlike strands.

COLUMELLA: The coiling axis of the shell of a snail.

CONCHOLOGY: The branch of zoology that studies the shells of mollusks.

DEXTRAL: See *sinistral*.

HERMAPHRODITE: An animal or plant having both male and female reproductive organs. Snails can be simultaneous hermaphrodites (for example, garden snails and sea slugs) or successive hermaphrodites (for example, slipper limpets).

MALACOLOGY: The branch of zoology that studies mollusks and their shells.

NEW SPECIES: A species not previously recognized by scientists as distinct from other species. The species is "new" to science, but not newly emerging on Earth.

NOMENCLATURE: The mechanism for applying names to living organisms and the rules that govern the application and use of these names.

OPERCULUM: The horny (or sometimes calcified) membrane that closes the shell of a mollusk when it is retracted inside. Not all mollusks have an operculum.

RADULA: A ribbon that carries the microscopic teeth that a mollusk uses to scrap, attack, or grind its food.

SINISTRAL: When a shell is held with its tip pointing upward and aperture facing the observer, the coiling is *sinistral* if the aperture is on the left. The opposite of *sinistral* is *dextral*, if the aperture is on the right. The vast majority of snails are *dextral*.

SIPHON: The part of the body of a clam or a snail that is used to funnel seawater in and out of the animal.

SYNONYM: One of two or more names used to designate the same species.

SYSTEMATICS: The branch of biology that describes and classifies living and fossil animals, plants, fungi, and microorganisms; also known as *taxonomy*.

VALVE: One of the two shells of clams; hence the term *bivalve* is used to designate them.

VARIX: A thickened element in the sculpture of a seashell.

WHORL: In a spirally coiled shell, one full turn of the spiral covering 360 degrees. Most snails have six to twelve whorls, although some have as many as forty.